CHARLES E. BRADFORD, D.D.

THE ABUNDANT LIFE
BIBLE
AMPLIFIER

TIMOTHY & TITUS

Counsels to Young Pastors
for Struggling Churches

GEORGE R. KNIGHT
General Editor

Pacific Press Publishing Association
Boise, Idaho
Oshawa, Ontario, Canada

Edited by Marvin Moore
Designed by Tim Larson
Typeset in 11/14 Janson Text

Library of Congress Cataloging-in-Publication Data:

Bradford, Charles E.
    Timothy & Titus : counsels to young pastors for struggling
churches / Charles E. Bradford.
        p.   cm. — (The Abundant life Bible amplifier)
    Includes bibliographical references.
    ISBN 0-8163-1213-3. — ISBN 0-8163-1215-X (pbk.)
    1. Bible. N. T. Pastoral Epistles—Criticism, interpretation,
etc. 2. Pastoral theology—Biblical teaching.   I. Title. II. Title:
Timothy and Titus. III. Series.
BS2735.2.B72   1994
227'.8307—dc20
                                                          93-50863
                                                              CIP

94 95 96 97 98 • 5 4 3 2 1

CONTENTS

General Preface 7
Author's Preface 9
How to Use This Book 11
Introduction to Timothy and Titus 15
List of Works Cited 21

Part I: 1 Timothy—Dealing With False Teachers
Introduction to 1 Timothy 27
  1. The Problem at Ephesus 31
  2. Counsels on Worship 44
  3. Counsels on the Well-ordered Community 59
  4. General Counsels 70
  5. Counsels on Social and Ethical Issues 81
  6. Parting Counsels 96

Part II: 2 Timothy—Passing the Torch
Introduction to 2 Timothy 111
  7. Passing on the Torch 114
  8. A Call to Commitment and Strength 125
  9. Facing Terrible Times 136

Part III: Titus—Crisis in Crete
Introduction to Titus 155
  10. Unfinished Business in Crete 158
  11. Teach These Things 169
  12. Doing What Is Good 180

GENERAL PREFACE

The Abundant Life Bible Amplifier series is aimed at helping readers understand the Bible better. Rather than merely offering comments on or about the Bible, each volume seeks to enable people to study their Bibles with fuller understanding.

To accomplish that task, scholars who are also proven communicators have been selected to author each volume. The basic idea underlying this combination is that scholarship and the ability to communicate on a popular level are compatible skills.

While the Bible Amplifier is written with the needs and abilities of laypeople in mind, it will also prove helpful to pastors and teachers. Beyond individual readers, the series will be useful in church study groups and as guides to enrich participation in the weekly prayer meeting.

Rather than focusing on the details of each verse, the Bible Amplifier series seeks to give readers an understanding of the themes and patterns of each biblical book as a whole and how each passage fits into that context. As a result, the series does not seek to solve all the problems or answer all the questions that may be related to a given text. In the process of accomplishing the goal for the series, both inductive and explanatory methodologies are used.

Each volume in this series presents its author's understanding of the biblical book being studied. As such, it does not necessarily represent the "official position" of the Seventh-day Adventist Church.

It should be noted that the Bible Amplifier series utilizes the New International Version of the Bible as its basic text. *Every reader should read the "How to Use This Book" section to get the fullest benefit from the Bible Amplifier volumes.*

Dr. Charles Bradford is uniquely qualified to develop the volume on the pastoral epistles for the Bible Amplifier series. Not only has he been a pastor and an evangelist for many years, but he has also been a conference president. His last full-time denominational position was as president of the North American Division of the Seventh-day Adventist church. Thus, throughout his extensive career, Dr. Bradford has not only fulfilled the role of a Timothy and a Titus, but also that of a Paul. More than just an administrator, "Brad" (as he is still affectionately called by all who know him) is a pastor's pastor. His broad practical experience does much to enrich his treatment of the pastoral epistles.

George R. Knight

AUTHOR'S PREFACE

The most urgent theological task before us today is to understand what the church is all about. The pastoral epistles provide marvelous insights into the nature and function of the church. We need all the intelligence that we can gather on the doctrine of the church—this "object of God's supreme regard." But the practical aspect of the problem—the "how to"—is always the most difficult. We must go beyond interpretation of Scripture to the application of Scripture.

Therefore, it becomes our common task to approach the doctrine of the church from every perspective—from every possible point of view. Together, as Christ's redeemed community, we must ponder the question, How is the church structured? How does it function? What are the dynamics at work in the body of Christ? We must come to view the church, not just as anatomy (organization and structure), but as physiology—an organism, a system. There must be wisdom and insight into how all this becomes "present truth." This is where the pastorals are so helpful—when we attempt to bridge the gap between the first century and our time to bring theory and practice together.

What continues to awaken my wonder and admiration is how Paul's examination and analysis of the challenges that the church faced in his time can be so appropriate to our situation. We can almost put present-day names, faces, and places into the text. However, the student must resist making applications before carefully and prayerfully examining the text. First comes the hard and sometimes tedious task of exegesis—listening to the text and understanding what it actually says and not just what we, at first glance, may think it says. Only after we have accomplished this will we be able to bring the Word to bear upon the local setting. We must be careful not to run before catching the ball!

These letters speak powerfully across the centuries. I am sure that the Holy Spirit will illumine us (this is His office work). We do need to read, reread, and meditate on the text until we feel we are there, until we become a part of the scene. Even then, we will need to look to the divine Interpreter to save us from misapplication of the Word—to help us "correctly handle the word of truth" (2 Tim. 2:15).

It has been my privilege over the past forty-seven years to look at the church up close. The church has been my life, my identity. I could not extricate myself from all this if I wanted to. I can only come at this study from a Seventh-day Adventist perspective. And while I have tried not to sermonize too much or "testify"—that is, to make my own experience the meaning of the text—this bias is bound to bleed through, at least a little. Pure objectivity is difficult to achieve. In this I ask to be forgiven. My fervent prayer is that nothing shall obscure the meaning of Scripture, "what the Spirit says to the churches" (Rev. 2:7).

The attempt to cover the entire Bible in this new series—The Abundant Life Bible Amplifier—is an ambitious undertaking indeed, and all of us, both authors and readers, are indebted to general editor George Knight and the Pacific Press for their willingness to venture this project. I am personally indebted to Dr. Knight for his careful reading of the manuscript and his many helpful suggestions.

Charles Bradford

How to Use This Book

The Abundant Life Bible Amplifier series treats each major portion of each Bible book in five main sections.

The first section is called "Getting Into the Word." The purpose of this section is to encourage readers to study their own Bibles. For that reason, the text of the Bible has not been printed in the volumes in this series.

You will get the most out of your study if you work through the exercises in each of the "Getting Into the Word" sections. This will not only aid you in learning more about the Bible but will also increase your skill in using Bible tools and in asking (and answering) meaningful questions about the Bible.

It will be helpful if you write out the answers and keep them in a notebook or file folder for each biblical book. Writing out your thoughts will enhance your understanding. The benefit derived from such study, of course, will be proportionate to the amount of effort expended.

The "Getting Into the Word" sections assume that the reader has certain minimal tools available. Among these are a concordance and a Bible with maps and marginal cross-references. If you don't have a New International Version of the Bible, we recommend that you obtain one for use with this series, since all the Bible Amplifier authors are using the NIV as their basic text. For the same reason, your best choice of a concordance is the *NIV Exhaustive Concordance*, edited by E. W. Goodrick and J. R. Kohlenberger. *Strong's Exhaustive Concordance of the Bible* and

Introduction to Timothy and Titus

Reading the pastoral epistles (1 and 2 Timothy and Titus) is like listening in on a conversation between the most distinguished person of the day in his or her profession and a couple of young chosen successors. You begin to realize that they are not just having a pleasant little chitchat. It's more like a last will and testament—serious dialogue that will make a difference. The torch is being passed, history is being made, and the conversation is all the more exciting because of the stature of the senior consultant.

This is where we are in the pastorals. We are taken into the most intimate correspondence between the person who has had the greatest influence on the formation of Christ's church and two of his most promising young protégés. We can only hear one side of the conversation, but this makes the listening all the more challenging, even demanding. We must listen more intently.

The apostle's overriding concern is for the local congregations. His best thought and counsel, his distilled wisdom, is for these little groups of believers—house churches—scattered throughout the empire. They are never out of his mind. "Besides everything else," Paul writes, "I face daily the pressure of my concern for all the churches" (2 Cor. 11:28). But he speaks to the congregations through these two young pastors. (In today's church Timothy and Titus would probably be called mission superintendents or conference presidents rather than pastors. I call them pastors because their ministry has to do with the care of souls.)

Paul charges Timothy and Titus with the welfare of the churches. These letters are called "pastoral epistles" because they are about the care and feeding of God's household.

Leadership—the Essential Ingredient

Paul addresses the pastors because their leadership is crucial. As the pastors go, so go the churches. Ellen White has said that "all branches of the work belong to the ministers," and "the efficiency of the church is precisely what the zeal, purity, self-denial, and the intelligent labor of the ministers make it" (*Testimonies for the Church*, 5:375, 582). Of course, pastors are not supercompetent by virtue of their ordination. The pastor is not a proprietor. He is a steward, entrusted with "God's work" (Titus 1:7). He exercises a representative ministry on behalf of the whole church and has an obligation to foster and support every department, every phase of church activity.

The pastoral epistles emphasize the importance of pure doctrine and dedicated leadership. Pastors must be examples to the flock in every respect—in family life and in relationships with others. Theirs is a teaching ministry, so they must have a good grasp of doctrine. What the people believe is important. According to Paul, false teachers and false doctrines are to be avoided like the plague. The servant of God must expose and rebuke heretics promptly and with severity. They must be shown up for what they are, because to follow them and their teachings is to make shipwreck of one's faith. Paul minces no words on this matter. He has no time for idle chatter, Jewish fables, or genealogies. Have nothing to do with these, he warns.

Counsel for Special Situations

Much of the counsel in the pastoral epistles has to do with specific situations in the churches that Timothy and Titus were responsible for. Because of this, these letters are difficult to systematize, to outline. They were written in the heat of battle, under intense pressure. They are rich, varied, far-ranging. Paul moves rapidly from one subject to another, from theme to theme. There are warnings, instructions, last-day scenarios, profiles of false teachers and faithful teachers, descriptions of real-life situations that must be met, heresies that must be unmasked, church members and even leaders who have to be rebuked.

Like case studies, the pastorals are written with people in mind and specific situations clearly in view. Paul did not write them as systematic presentations of doctrines. In the case of 1 Timothy, Paul hopes to be in Ephesus soon, but if not, "You will know how people ought to conduct themselves in the house of God" (3:15). And to Titus he dashes off a memo instructing the young preacher to bind off the work on Crete and make his way to Nicopolis. Paul wrote 2 Timothy from prison to prepare the young preacher to face the future with its spiraling pressures confidently, when there is no Paul to lean on.

This is not to say that the pastorals are a church manual with no theological value. Rich statements of faith can be found all through these letters, along with at least two beautiful hymns of devotion to Christ. But doctrine is not their main thrust.

In order for the church to survive, there must be greater discipline and structure. The situation calls for applied theology, practical theology. Paul's great interest is the survival and preservation of the church in a hostile environment.

In our study we shall try to get into Paul's thinking as he wrote. What did he have in mind when he made some of those puzzling statements that are "hard to be understood"? Is he laying down hard and fast law when he speaks about slaves or the position of women? How are we to take his assessment of the terrible Cretans (Titus 1:12, 13)? To what extent are his counsels directed to specific and local situations? We need to find out all we can about Paul's world, its people, customs, morals, family life, politics, social life, burning issues—the times when the counsels were given.

We do not know exactly when the pastoral epistles were written, or even in what order they were written. Some scholars think that Titus was written first. It is almost certain that 2 Timothy was Paul's final letter, penned in sight of the execution chamber, most likely in the late A.D. 60s. The churches had been organized long enough to have a track record, to have gone through a variety of experiences.

Some scholars think the pastorals were written much later (well after A.D. 100), because, in their view, they seem to address a more fully developed, more highly organized church than the simple house churches of the last third of the first century. Such scholars feel the writer is addressing heresies that developed much later than Paul's day. This, it should be noted, is "their" view. Societal developments do not always require long evolutionary periods of time. Church historians are finding to their amazement how soon the church fell into apostasy. It should also be understood that church organization developed quite rapidly. Jesus began the process with the ordination of the twelve, and by the time of the writing of Acts, the Jerusalem church was thoroughly organized. Early on, the New Testament church had a full complement of officers (ministering servants) in place, affirmed by the congregations.

Common Dangers—Paul's Day and Ours

The church has always lived under constant threat and present danger. Whether active persecution or the danger of being swallowed up by the prevailing culture, the threats are real. But the dangers from within are the most insidious. "I know that after I leave," Paul declared, "savage wolves will come in among you and will not spare the flock. Even from your own number men will arise and distort truth in order to draw away disciples after them" (Acts 20:29, 30).

Each of the pastoral epistles urges vigilance against the inroads of false teachers and false doctrines. If the apostle seems almost paranoid on this point, it is because he sees the dangers all the more clearly. He must vigorously sound the alarm in no uncertain terms. This is the compelling reason for the pastoral epistles. Experienced Christians can identify with Paul's insistent warnings. The church will always have those in its midst who crave positions of leadership, and when they are not chosen, will appoint themselves and work with fanatical zeal to get their ideas before the church as a whole in order to gain a following. This is why the pastoral epistles are so relevant for every age and why they are increasingly applicable to the modern church.

Scripture a Bulwark

The urgent question before us is, How shall we do Scripture? How do we make 2,000-year-old counsels up-to-date and relevant? This question is fundamental, unavoidable. The Bible's message is both general and specific—to the whole people of God and to each individual believer. We cannot get beyond it or outgrow our need of it. The Word builds, strengthens, and fortifies the Christian against the ever-present dangers. There is wisdom and common sense in what the prophets have to say. The Holy Spirit chose the pastoral epistles for inclusion in the canon of Scripture because of their teaching and saving values for us today.

Thomas C. Oden points out that "the Pastorals are 'third generation' correspondence. The second was represented by Timothy's mother, Eunice, and the first by his grandmother, Lois. Young Timothy and Titus were among the best representatives of that third generation" (Oden, 1). But again, how do we get at them? How do we bring them closer to our day? Certainly not by any freewheeling, irresponsible surface treatment. "God," Oletta Wald says, "has placed a price on the deep treasures of His Word: the price is prayer, meditation, a willingness to spend the time to think, to search, to study. Whether you scratch the surface in your Bible study or whether you dig deeply into the message—all depends on how much time, energy, prayer and discipline you put into it" (Wald, 51).

The purpose and objective of the matter actually is not to master the rules and methods of interpretation so much as it is to find the Word and to "eat it." "The correct interpretation of the scriptures," Ellen White points out, "is not all that God requires. He enjoins upon us that we should not only know the truth, but that we should practice the truth as it is in Jesus" (*1888 Materials*, 1:201).

The perfect spiritual formation of the church is the ultimate goal. It is to be "a radiant church, without stain or wrinkle or any other blemish, but holy and blameless" (Eph. 5:27). Because that goal was not yet realized, the apostle was in "birth pangs." But he lived in hope because he knew the mature formation of the church was the will of "our great God and Savior, Jesus Christ, who gave himself for us to redeem us from all wickedness and to purify for himself a people that are his very own, eager to do what is good" (Titus 2:13, 14).

■ Further Study of the Word

1. For more information on Paul's letters to Timothy and Titus, see Francis O. Nichol, ed., *Seventh-day Adventist Bible Dictionary*, s.v. "Timothy, Epistles To" and "Titus, Epistle To."
2. For more on the life of Timothy, see Ellen G. White, *The Acts of the Apostles*, 184, 185, 202-204.
3. For general background information, see William Barclay, *The Letters to Timothy, Titus, and Philemon*, 1-6.
4. On inductive Bible study, see Oletta Wald, *The Joy of Discovery*, 6, 7, 9, 51, 52.

WORKS CITED

Achtemeier, Paul J. ed. *Harper's Bible Dictionary*. San Francisco: Harper and Row, 1985.

Arndt, William F., and F. Wilbur Gingrich. *A Greek Lexicon of the New Testament*. Chicago: University of Chicago Press, 1958.

Balz, Horst, and Gerhard Shneider, eds. *Exegetical Dictionary of the New Testament*. Grand Rapids, Mich.: William B. Eerdmans, 1993.

Banks, Rosa Taylor, ed. *A Woman's Place*. Hagerstown, Md.: Review and Herald, 1992.

Barclay, William. *The Letters to Timothy, Titus, and Philemon*. Philadelphia: Westminster, 1975.

Barker, Glenn W., and William L. Lane. *The New Testament Speaks*. New York: Harper and Row, 1969.

Beker, J. Christiaan. *Paul the Apostle*. Philadelphia: Fortress, 1980.

Bradford, Charles E. *The God Between*. Hagerstown, Md.: Review and Herald, 1984.

Bromiley, Geoffrey W., ed. *International Standard Bible Encyclopedia*, rev. ed., 4 vols. Grand Rapids, Mich.: Eerdmans, 1979-1988.

Bruce, F. F. *The First Epistle to the Corinthians*. Grand Rapids, Mich.: William B. Eerdmans, 1987.

_____ *Paul: Apostle of the Heart Set Free*. Grand Rapids, Mich.: Eerdmans, 1977.

Charlesworth, James H. *Jesus Within Judaism*. New York: Doubleday, 1988.

Conn, Keith, general ed. *Abingdon Dictionary of Living Religions*. Nashville: Abingdon, 1981.

De Pree, Max. *Leadership Is an Art*. New York: Dell, 1989.

Dibelius, Martin, and Hans Conzelmann. *The Pastoral Epistles*. Hermenia Commentaries. Philadelphia: Fortress, 1972.

Dudley, Roger, and Bailey Gillespie. *Valuegenesis: Faith in the Balance*. Riverside, Calif.: La Sierra University Press, 1992.

Dulles, Avery. *Models of the Church*. New York: Doubleday, 1987.

Evans, Roger S. "A Biblical Theology of Drinking." *Ministry*, July 1993, 12.

Fee, Gordon D. *1 and 2 Timothy, Titus*. New International Bible Commentary. Peabody, Mass.: Hendrickson, 1988.

Guthrie, Donald. *The Pastoral Epistles*. Tyndale New Testament Commentaries. Grand Rapids, Mich.: Eerdmans, 1990.

Hall, Douglas John. *Stewardship of Life in the Kingdom of Death*. Grand Rapids, Mich.: Eerdmans, 1988.

Harper's Bible Dictionary. San Francisco: Harper and Row, 1985.

Hawthorne, Gerald F. and Roger P. Martin, eds. *Dictionary of Paul and His Letters*. Downers Grove, Ill.: InterVarsity, 1993.

Hendricksen, William. *Thessalonians, Timothy and Titus*. Grand Rapids, Mich.: Baker, 1979.

Horn, Siegfried H., et. al. *Seventh-day Adventist Bible Dictionary*, rev. ed., edited by Raymond H. Woolsey. Hagerstown, Md.: Review and Herald, 1979.

Kelly, Geffrey B., and F. Burton Nelson, eds. *A Testament to Freedom: The Essential Writings of Dietrich Bonhoeffer*. San Francisco: Harper San Francisco, 1990.

Layton, Bentley, trans. *The Gnostic Scriptures*. Garden City, N.Y.: Doubleday, 1987.

Lea, Thomas D., and Hayne P. Griffin, Jr. "The Sons of the Martyr," in *1, 2 Timothy, Titus*. The New American Commentary, vol. 34. Nashville: Broadman Press, 1992.

Markus, Barth. *Ephesians*. The Anchor Bible, vol. 34a. Garden City, N.J.: Doubleday, 1974.

Neufeld, Don, ed. *Seventh-day Adventist Encyclopedia*. Washington, D.C.: Review and Herald, 1976.

_____*Seventh-day Adventist Source Book*. Washington, D.C.: Review and Herald, 1962.

Nichol, Frances D. *Answers to Objections*. Washington, D.C.: Review and Herald, 1952.

_____, ed. *Seventh-day Adventist Bible Commentary* (*SDABC*), 7 vols. Washington, D.C.: Review and Herald, 1953-1957.

Oden, Thomas C. *First and Second Timothy and Titus*. Louisville, Ky.: John Knox, 1989.

Olsen, V. Norskov. *Myth and Truth—Church, Priesthood and Ordination*. Riverside, Calif.: Loma Linda University Press, 1990.

Quinn, Jerome D. *The Letter to Titus*. Anchor Bible, vol. 35. New York: Doubleday, 1990.

Sandmel, Samuel. *Judaism and Christian Beginnings*. London: Oxford University Press, 1978.

Schweitzer, Frederick. *A History of the Jews*. New York: MacMillan, 1971.

Seventh-day Adventist Church Manual. Washington, D.C.: General Conference of Seventh-day Adventists, 1986.   ,

Seventh-day Adventists Answer Questions on Doctrine. Washington, D.C.: Review and Herald, 1957.

Seventh-day Adventists Believe . . . : A Biblical Exposition of 27 Fundamental Doctrines. Washington, D.C.: Ministerial Association, General Conference of Seventh-day Adventists, 1988.

Thompson, Alden. *Inspiration*. Hagerstown, Md.: Review and Herald, 1991.

Van Dolson, Leo R. *Hidden No Longer*. Boise, Idaho: Pacific Press, 1968.

Vine, W. E. *An Expository Dictionary of New Testament Words*. Old Tappan, N.J.: Fleming and Revell, 1966.

Wald, Oletta. *The Joy of Discovery*. Minneapolis: Bible Banner, 1956.

Whistan, William, trans. *Josephus Complete Works*. Grand Rapids, Mich.: Kregel, 1963.

White, Ellen G. *The Acts of the Apostles*. Boise, Idaho: Pacific Press, 1911.

_____*Christian Leadership*. Washington, D.C.: Ellen G. White Estate, 1974.

_____*Christian Service*. General Conference of Seventh-day Adventists, 1947.

_____*Testimonies for the Church*, 9 vols. Boise, Idaho: Pacific Press, 1948.

This volume on Titus and Timothy refers to several other works by Ellen White that are not included in this list.

PART ONE

1 Timothy

Dealing With
False Teachers

Introduction to
1 Timothy

One of the best ways to study a book of the Bible is to read it thoughtfully from beginning to end as quickly as possible. In the case of the pastoral epistles, this will not involve a great deal of time. The following suggestions will help you to get the most out of a thoughtful reading of 1 Timothy:

1. **Paul's first letter to Timothy is filled with counsel for dealing with problems in the church at Ephesus. As you read through his letter, see how many of these problems you can identify. Especially watch for ideas that might help your church solve some of its problems.**
2. **While 1 Timothy is primarily practical advice for a pastor, Paul also drops in theological insights and helpful hints about daily living. Make a list of these as you read, and ask yourself how they might have helped Timothy to deal with the problems he faced in the church at Ephesus. How can they help you in your own Christian life and in your relationship to your local church?**
3. **If 1 Timothy were the only book in the Bible that said anything about God, what important lessons would you learn?**

Paul has left Timothy in Ephesus, where serious problems threaten the church. The "savage wolves" (false teachers) Paul had predicted would arise, who "will not spare the flock" (Acts 20:29), are out in full force. In order to meet this clear and present danger, the young Timothy needs strength of character—toughness, fortitude. He needs good judgment and insight into human

27

nature. Most of all, he needs the guidance of the Holy Spirit.

The Ephesian believers, newly converted from paganism, need strong pastoral leadership. In the spiritual as well as in the physical world, the newborn need constant care. They have experienced new life, but because they are still in fleshly bodies, there is the incessant tug of the old life. Experienced gospel workers know that as the struggle intensifies, new believers often experience "buyer's regret." False teachers take advantage of this circumstance. Timothy must act promptly and decisively to save those who have newly come to life in Christ.

Timothy may be young, but he is not a novice. He has served his internship with the great apostle and has gained his confidence (Acts 16:1-5). He has a thorough grasp of Scripture (2 Tim. 3:15). Converted under Paul's preaching at Lystra, he was probably among those who stood by the apostle's bruised body when he was stoned and dragged, almost lifeless, out of the city (Acts 14:19, 20). We know that Timothy was a ministerial associate of Paul's in Berea (Acts 17:13, 14), and probably at Athens (Acts 17:15), at Philippi (Phil. 2:19-24), at Corinth (Acts 18:2, 5), in Macedonia (Acts 19:22), and in Thessalonica (1 Thess. 3:2, 6).

The veteran apostle has great confidence in his junior associate and feels very close to him, to the extent that he joins Timothy's name with his own in greetings and salutations in six of his epistles (2 Corinthians, Philippians, Colossians, 1 and 2 Thessalonians, and Philemon). He endorses Timothy to the Corinthian church: "See to it that he has nothing to fear while he is with you, for he is carrying on the work of the Lord, just as I am. No one, then, should refuse to accept him" (1 Cor. 16:10, 11). Paul has no doubt that Timothy is the right person for the Ephesian situation.

However, knowing the young pastor's temperament, the apostle feels constrained to constantly challenge him to use his authority, to be more forthright, less laid-back. The right use of authority requires great wisdom, but Timothy is not to refrain from using his authority merely because he is young (1:3; 6:17, 18).

Timothy's task is complicated by the presence of false teachers in the church. Some of them are former believers and even associates in ministry. This explains their bitterness and determination to wreak havoc on the young churches. The situation could hardly be more serious—even grim.

This letter was not written from prison. We know this from the fact that several times Paul mentions his desire to visit Timothy (3:14, 15; 4:13). Obviously, he was free to travel. At the time he wrote this letter, he was either in Macedonia or *en route* to Nicopolis.

Two major emphases stand out in 1 Timothy: threats to the church from false teachers and their teachings, and how to meet those threats doctrinally and organizationally. Paul characterizes the false teachers very clearly. They promote controversies and are overly self-confident (1:4, 7). They are hypocritical, liars, conscience-seared, and attempt to control people's personal lives and lifestyles (4:2, 3). They are conceited, devoid of understanding, have an unhealthy interest in controversies and arguments, and are out for financial gain (6:4). What a scathing indictment!

And what is the content of their teaching? Myths, endless genealogies, meaningless talk (1:3, 6); godless myths and old wives tales (4:7); godless chatter; and false knowledge (6:20). (See also 2 Tim. 2:16; 3:4; Titus 1:14; 3:9). The best cure for heresy is sound doctrine. That is why Paul places such a premium on the services of leaders, especially those who are able to preach and teach well (5:17).

In 1 Timothy Paul outlines a survival strategy for struggling young churches: meet doctrinal problems head on with the Word; expose false teachers; choose only the tried and true for leadership responsibilities; give these trusted servants good support. Good organization is also a protection. Worship must be orderly. Families are to discipline themselves. A struggling church does not need—indeed, cannot afford—the reputation of being unstable. The gospel is recommended by the believers' sensible, responsible demeanor, and there will be no occasion for reproach. The critics' mouths will be stopped. Even magistrates and rulers will recognize and appreciate Christians as solid citizens and a credit to the community.

Paul's first letter to Timothy was not written in a vacuum. It was framed with a particular background, setting, and purpose in mind. With this understanding, we will be able to more fully comprehend the counsel to his young protégé.

Outline of 1 Timothy

I. Salutation (1:1, 2)
   A. Identity and authority of the author (1:1)
   B. Identity of the recipient (1:2)
II. Warning against false teachers (1:3-11)
   A. Command them not to teach false doctrines (1:3-7)
   B. The right use of the law (1:8-11)
III. God's grace to Paul (1:12-20)
   A. From blasphemer to apostle (1:12, 13)
   B. Abundant grace and mercy (1:14-17)
   C. Danger of departure from the faith (1:18-20)
IV. Instructions concerning worship (2:1-15)
   A. The church a praying community (2:1-7)
   B. Men at prayer (2:8)
   C. Women at prayer (2:9-15)
V. Overseers and deacons (3:1-16)
   A. Qualifications and lifestyle of overseers (3:1-7)
   B. Of deacons (3:8-10, 12, 13)
   C. Of deaconesses (3:11)
   D. Behavior in the house of God (3:14, 15)
   E. The mystery of godliness (3:16)
VI. Instructions to Timothy (4:1-16)
   A. Last-day deceptions (4:1-5)
   B. Command and teach (4:6-14)
   C. Diligence and watchfulness (4:15, 16)
VII. Advice about various groups (5:1–6:2)
   A. Treatment of brothers and sisters (5:1, 2)
   B. Widows (5:3-16)
   C. Elders (5:17-20)
   D. General instructions (5:21-25)
   E. Slaves (6:1, 2)
VIII. Warning against the love of money (6:3-10)
   A. Teaching for gain (6:3-5)
   B. True gain (6:6-8)
   C. Riches a snare (6:9, 10)
IX. Charge to Timothy (6:11-20)
   A. Things to avoid and to pursue (6:11-16)
   B. Additional commands to the rich (6:17-19)
   C. Guard what has been entrusted (6:20, 21)

CHAPTER ONE

The Problem at Ephesus: Dealing With False Teachers

1 Timothy 1

At the beginning of his first letter to Timothy, Paul clarifies his reason for writing: false teachers. He has left Timothy in Ephesus to address this problem. The strategy he recommends is to "command certain men not to teach false doctrines any longer" (vs. 3). The apostle does not spend a lot of time in a long introduction. He comes quickly to the point: "Deal with the false teachers."

■ Getting Into the Word

After reading the first chapter of 1 Timothy two times, reflect on the following questions:

1. Since the first letter to Timothy addresses the situation in Ephesus (1:3), it will be helpful to learn as much as we can about that city. Read the article on Ephesus in the *Seventh-day Adventist Bible Dictionary*. Also locate the city on the map in the back of your Bible or in a Bible atlas. Acts 18:23–19:41 will also help you to understand the situation that Paul and Timothy faced. What impression does that passage leave you with concerning the city of Ephesus and the difficulties and possibilities of doing ministry there?

2. Later, Paul's itinerary took him to Miletus—a coastal community near Ephesus. From here, Paul sent for the Ephesian elders and preached a significant prophetic message about the dangers they would face in the near

future (Acts 20:17-38). Read that sermon, noticing especially the prophecy in verses 29, 30. In what ways does a reading of this passage shed light on the situation in Ephesus at the time Paul wrote 1 Timothy?

3. In 1 Timothy 1:3-7 Paul enumerates the character flaws and problems of the false teachers. Make a list of these problems. What, according to Paul, will be the outcome if the situation is allowed to go unchecked? How will the church and its fellowship be affected?

4. In verses 8 and 9 Paul intimates that God's law may be used unlawfully. In what ways is that true? (Rom. 3:23; 4:15; 7:7 will be helpful here.)

5. Verses 12 to 16 are a powerful statement on the operation of God's grace. What did Paul consider to be the most convincing evidence that the grace of God is effective in changing human lives? What is the relationship between God's mercy and His grace? What words and expressions does Paul use to indicate the adequacy of God's saving action? What singular powers of the Deity does Paul delineate in verse 17? In what ways does his concept of God shape Paul's understanding of grace and mercy? What Old Testament ideas of God's majesty and power come through in this passage?

■ Exploring the Word

Apostolic Authority

Even apostles need credentials. Leaders need authentication. The people have a right to know—by whose authority does a certain person speak? Paul is not hesitant to present his credentials. He is "an apostle of Jesus Christ" (1:1).

The Greek word *apostolos* (English: *apostle*) provides an example of how New Testament writers appropriated secular words—often obscure words—from their culture and invested them with distinctively Christian meaning. In classical Greek *apostolos* referred to a naval expedition, and possibly its commander as well. It could mean a ship ready for departure and probably came to mean "sending out." In the New Testament an apostle is one who is sent. He has ambassadorial status. He is the authorized representative of the Sender. In Paul's view, the one sent was regarded as the person of the one who sent him.

Thus at the very outset, in the salutation, Paul establishes his position. He is an apostle—he was sent—"by the command of God" (vs. 1). The Greek word translated as command is *epitagē*—a royal injunction, inviolable orders from the king. It included the command from the king and the instructions that came with the commission. The emissary was thus clothed with authority.

Even though Paul speaks to Timothy in very warm personal terms as his "son in the faith" (vs. 2), his letter is more than a personal note. While it is addressed to Timothy, it is intended for the entire community of faith. It is to be taken seriously. And while apostles are human beings, fellow servants, and must not lord it over the flock, their message and mission is authoritative and vital to the welfare of the church of the living God.

Strictly speaking, the number of apostles was limited to those disciples who were associated with Christ in His ministry, eyewitnesses to His passion, and by His appointment made founders of the Christian church. In this sense the ministry of the apostles was unique and came to a close with the last of the original group of eyewitnesses. But Paul was convinced that he was qualified as an apostle because of his Damascus-road confrontation with the living Christ. He received his commission personally from "Christ Jesus our hope" (vs. 1).

All the New Testament epistles begin in much the same way as any other first-century correspondence. There is a greeting, a salutation, a personal word, etc. But these letters are distinctive in that they always begin with reference to the kingdom of God, His work on earth, the family of believers in Christ, etc. "Grace, mercy and peace from God the Father and Christ Jesus our Lord" (vs. 2), Paul says.

False Teachers and Their Teaching

Primary reason for the letter. Immediately following the greeting comes Paul's primary reason for writing the letter: "As I urged you when I went into Macedonia, stay there in Ephesus so that

line, or "the goal," as Paul puts it in verse 5 (Greek *telos*), is love "which comes from a pure heart and a good conscience and a sincere faith." Throughout the pastorals Paul focuses on outcomes, results, effects.

What is the "pure heart" that he spoke about? The ancients assigned tremendous moral, emotional, and intellectual significance to the term *heart*. "Above all else, guard your heart," said the wise man, "for it is the wellspring of life" (Prov. 4:23). Purity as used here suggests being cleansed or having been cleansed. "Create in me a pure heart, O God" (Ps. 51:10) was David's sincere prayer. Ellen White's comment is to the point: "When it is in the heart to obey God, when efforts are put forth to this end, Jesus accepts this disposition and effort as man's best service, and He makes up for the deficiency with His own divine merit" (*Selected Messages*, 1:382).

The "pure heart" is marked by humility. This quality is foreign to the very nature of the false teachers, who continue to be fascinated by "meaningless talk" (vs. 6). They crave the title Doctor of the Law, but they have never paid their dues. They speak well and are ready to expand on all kinds of subjects but are really unqualified. Jesus' indictment of the Pharisees applies: "You are in error because you do not know the Scriptures or the power of God" (Matt. 22:29). Two basic qualifications exist for the religious teacher: knowledge of Scripture and the experience of the transforming power of God in the life.

Proper Use of the Law

The false teachers have already displayed serious character flaws, and it is predictable that they will pervert the purpose and proper use of the law. "The law is good if a man uses it properly," Paul said (vs. 8). The nature and function of law is of great significance. What does Paul mean by the terms *law, the law, God's law?* At times in his writings he is referring to the Ten Commandments, the moral law. In other instances he means the sum total of instruction from God, the Old Testament Scriptures. Paul has no restricted, narrowed-down view of law.

Adventists have tended to separate the law into its moral, ceremonial, and civil aspects. This is helpful, but the biblical writers do not always make such neat distinctions. The law in Galatians was a much-debated subject among Adventists in the 1880s and 1890s. The burning question was, Is it the moral law or the ceremonial law? We finally came to see that the apostle was speaking of both the moral and ceremonial aspects of law.

Law in all its forms is a statement about God, His character, His person. The law is a transcript of God's character, and it is good. "So then, the law is holy, and the commandment is holy, righteous and good" (Rom. 7:12). This is the positive side.

There is also a negative side. Whatever is out of kilter with God's law comes under His judgment. In its negative expression, the law is a terror to evildoers. It was given by a gracious God as a check and barrier to sin. It points out sin, warns against transgression, sets boundaries, draws lines.

Wherever we see the law spoken of in the Bible, we must look at the context to determine its meaning. In verses 9 and 10 it seems clear that Paul is referring almost exclusively to the moral law, the Ten Commandments. It was made "for murderers, for adulterers and perverts, for slave traders and liars and perjurers"—to put, as we say, the fear of God in them, to turn them around, to arrest them.

One thing is certain; false teachers do not know the nature of the law or its function. Because the law is spiritual, it rules out "whatever else is contrary to the sound doctrine" (vs. 10). Even the law, however, must conform to the "glorious gospel of the blessed God" (vs. 11).

The law is not a method of salvation—it is not an instrument of salvation. Salvation does not come through law. Grace is the method of salvation. There is, however, no conflict between law and grace or law and gospel. Both work together. We must maintain a balance in our teaching of the law. To make the law an instrument of salvation leads to legalism. This is contrary to the gospel, which clearly states that we are saved by grace. On the other hand, if we set aside the law and try to make grace a standard, we fall into antinomianism (opposition to law), which literally means "against law."

The debate over law has gone on for centuries, and sometimes the church has lurched to one extreme or the other. Every teaching and practice must be brought into perfect conformity to the law and the gospel—"the glorious gospel of the blessed God" (vs. 11).

When Paul speaks of the blessed God, he is speaking of the One from whom all blessings flow, whose attitude toward His earthborn children is always one of grace. This is the kind of gospel—good news—which has been entrusted to him, and he wants to pass it on to his son Timothy for the church as a whole. Sound doctrine always gives equal time to law and gospel. "The law is good if a man uses it properly" (vs. 8).

God's Grace in Operation—His Unlimited Patience

Paul looked on himself as exhibit number one of God's amazing grace, His power to save. Otherwise, how could he, a former blasphemer and persecutor of the church, be made a minister of the gospel?

Blasphemy has to do with speech. To blaspheme is to injure with words, to revile, to rail against. Paul had used his tremendous theological knowledge to oppose Christ and His church. He had used all the power of the Sanhedrin to physically punish the Christians. That God could turn him around and make him an apostle, a co-worker with Him, was evidence of what He could do with all of humanity. He (Paul) was shown mercy, he says, because he acted in ignorance and unbelief. He is not excusing his actions. He is emphasizing that it is God's grace, His unlimited patience, that made it all possible.

In his exultation the apostle points out that the grace of our Lord was "poured out on me abundantly, along with the faith and love that are in Christ Jesus" (vs. 14). Paul's use of the word *faith* is worth our study. It is interesting to note that he couples faith with love. In an earlier letter Paul said to the Galatians, "The only thing that counts is faith expressing itself through love" (Gal. 5:6). The King James Version says, "Faith which worketh by love." The idea here is that faith must be active. Genuine faith works—it expresses itself—through love in concrete acts and deeds. Biblical faith never remains in the abstract.

The apostle assigns faith and love, along with hope (1 Cor. 13:13), the highest places in the scale of Christian virtues. The source of all Christian values, of course, is Christ Jesus. In verse 15 Paul drives home again this powerful truth in one of his trustworthy sayings, "Christ Jesus came into the world to save sinners—of whom I am the worst." Again and again he comes back to God's grace, His unlimited patience in action. The worst of sinners is shown mercy and becomes "an example for those who would believe on him and receive eternal life" (vs. 16).

Five times in the pastoral epistles Paul uses the phrase "Here is a trustworthy saying." It can also be translated as "faithful saying." In the vernacular we would say, "You can count on that," or "You can bet on that" (see also 3:1; 4:9; 2 Tim. 2:11; Titus 3:8). At this stage of his ministry, and at this point in the development of the church, Paul is beginning to place more emphasis on a body of doctrines—orthodoxy, if you please. The trustworthy sayings have universal application among the churches. They are for all times and all places.

What is this first universal reality or trustworthy saying? "Jesus Christ came into the world to save sinners, of whom I am the worst." The New Testament definition of a sinner is quite different from that of the religious leaders of the day. In their thinking, anyone who was not an Israelite or law keeper was a sinner. It was always other nations, other people, who were the sinners. The Pauline and New Testament definition of the sinner is universally applicable: "All have sinned and fall short of the glory of God" (Rom. 3:23). We call the other person a sinner, but God declares that all of us are sinners—the accuser as well as the accused!

To the King Eternal—a Doxology

In verse 17 the apostle is caught up in a doxology, a hymn of praise to the Creator God, the God of limitless grace. This God of boundless patience is the "King eternal, immortal, invisible, the only God." This is the God of eternity—infinite, limitless. His existence is outside of and beyond finite time. This God is ultimate and absolute. All is ascribed to Him. The language is as powerful and as emphatic as it could possibly be. Honor and glory

CHAPTER TWO

Counsels on Worship

1 Timothy 2

Chapter 2 introduces a long section in which Paul discusses a wide range of counsels encompassing various aspects of church and family life at Ephesus. In these counsels, which continue through chapter 6:2, Paul advises Timothy on such issues as the selection of church leaders, erroneous teachings on marriage and diet, the care of widows, and the relationship between slaves and masters. Sprinkled throughout this abundance of practical advice we will find some beautiful gems of theological insight that delightfully illumine the discussion.

In chapter 2 he directs his counsels to the church at worship. He advises the church about prayer for kings and rulers, and he gives specific admonition for both men and women about their attitude in prayer. He also gives specific advice to women on dress and adornment that has been important to Adventists for many years. And he will advise Timothy on the submission of women to men—an issue that has gained some prominence among Adventists in recent years.

■ Getting Into the Word

After you have read chapter 2 through at least two times, ask yourself the following questions:

1. Read about Jewish worship in the article entitled "Synagogue" in the *Seventh-day Adventist Bible Dictionary*. Keeping in mind that early Christian worship grew out of the synagogue experience, what allusions to synagogue worship do you find in 1 Timothy 2?

2. In verse 1 Paul encourages the members of the church in Ephesus to engage in intercessory prayer. Look up 1 John 2:1; Hebrews 7:25; and Romans 8:34, which speak of Christ's work as our Intercessor. In the Old Testament, look up the intercessory prayers of Moses and Daniel (Exod. 32:11-14, 31-34; Dan. 9:4-19). How is our intercessory praying to be like Christ's? How is ours different from His?

3. First Timothy 2:11-15 records one of Paul's most often quoted passages on the role of women in public worship. Compare his advice in 1 Timothy 2 with 1 Corinthians 11:5-15. What is the relationship between his counsel to the church at Ephesus and his counsel to the church at Corinth? What circumstances at Ephesus might have prompted Paul's counsel to that congregation? What is the relationship between this passage and such passages as Acts 18:26 and Joel 2:28-32? What do these passages say that can guide us in our discussions about the ordination of women?

■ Exploring the Word

The Church a Praying Community

At the outset Paul urges the church to pray (vs. 1). He sees this as a matter of high priority. Prayer is the hallmark of the authentic Christian community. Verse 1 indicates that he has the setting of public worship in mind, where the first order of business is prayer. The church has been given the ministry of intercessory prayer, and it must engage in that ministry. By offering up prayers, believers share in the priestly ministry of Christ (Heb. 13:15; 1 Pet. 2:5). They are to make earnest requests, humble entreaties, intercessions, and petitions with thanksgiving. Paul addresses the church as a priesthood of believers, *both male and female*, who have gathered for worship. He wants them to know what is required of them so that they may carry out their priestly functions in a manner that is pleasing to God (vs. 3).

Paul begins by urging that Christians are to pray "for everyone." The universality of the gospel and the church's global mission have always been uppermost in Paul's thinking. Therefore, these prayers are not to be narrow and exclusive. The church cannot allow itself to become obsessed with internal affairs. The spirit of the gospel is inclusive. All conditions, people, and situations are the legitimate objects of the Christian's prayers. Christians are the most cosmopolitan of people. The whole world is their parish.

In verse 2 the apostle gets more specific about whom Christians should pray for: "Kings and all those in authority" or high station. In his day this would have included the emperor, provincial officials, and local magistrates. The early Christians were encouraged to recognize the legitimacy and the necessity of secular government (see also Rom. 13:1-7; 1 Pet. 2:13-17). Even an oppressive government is better than anarchy. Rulers and officials are often cruel and tyrannical. They pass unjust laws. Nevertheless, it is the Christian's duty to pray for the welfare of all those persons who have the responsibility of governing. We should pray for the conversion of our rulers, and we should pray that they will be kindly disposed toward the Christian community and its mission. Believers must live under all kinds of political systems. The church's mission must go forward under the most adverse conditions, even in times of trouble.

Paul's deeper reason for urging Christians to pray for government leaders is "that we may live peaceful and quiet lives" (vs. 2). Jerome Quinn's translation says, "Our purpose is to spend a tranquil and quiet existence in an altogether godly and reverent way" (Quinn, 32). Paul had a fatherly care for the churches, and he wanted those conditions to exist that would be most ideal to their spiritual growth and the spreading of the gospel message. He recognized, of course, that persecution and trial are to be expected, for he himself said that "everyone who wants to live a godly life in Christ Jesus will be persecuted" (2 Tim. 3:12). But Christians are not to invite trouble. Their prayer should always be, "Lead us not into temptation."

This good life must not be spent idly and selfishly. There is a work of inreach (character development) and a work of outreach (witness to the world) to be done. There is a vital relationship between the two spheres. Avery Dulles states it well: "But it would not be completely Church unless it went forth from its assemblies to carry on Christ's work in the world. The Church's existence is a continual alternation between two phases. Like systole and diastole in the movement of the heart, like inhalation and exhalation in the process of breathing, assembly and mission succeed each other in the life of the Church. Discipleship would be stunted unless it included both the centripetal phase of worship and the centrifugal phase of mission" (Dulles, 220). All things being equal, both aspects of the believer's life are best developed under conditions of peace and stability.

Christians are to live peaceful and quiet lives "in all godliness and holiness" (vs. 2). Godliness is a life that properly reverences God with dignity. Holiness includes an inner condition of the heart that affects outward behavior. *Piety* is a good old-fashioned word that captures the sense of what the apostle is saying. The spiritual formation of the church as Christ's community and the lifestyle and demeanor of its individual believers is a powerful witness in favor of the religion of Jesus Christ in a hostile world. Even kings and magistrates are influenced. Most of all, the holy lives of His people are pleasing to God.

Paul also keeps the missionary purpose of the church at the front end of his argument. God has an intense longing for "all men to be saved and to come to a knowledge of the truth" (vs. 4). The salvation of Jews, Greeks, Romans, and barbarians is His will. Paul is not teaching universalism (the doctrine that all persons will ultimately be saved). The Bible clearly teaches that the human agent must respond to the promptings of the Spirit.

Seventh-day Adventists lean toward Armenianism (the doctrine of free will) more than to Calvinism in its extreme form (the fixed predestination of every human to salvation or condemnation). We must be careful, however, not to oversimplify the matter. The freedom of choice that God grants human beings does not diminish His Sovereignty. Ultimately, God's purposes will be fulfilled. The final outcome of the conflict between good and evil is assured regardless of what we do or the choices we make.

The Mediator

Paul now points out a truth that God wants all human beings to know: there is one God (vs. 5). The concept of the one God was Judaism's distinctive theological statement (Deut. 6:4). However, early in the biblical account we find the suggestion that God is a unity of more than one being: "Then God said, 'Let *us* make man' " (Gen. 1:26).

Yahweh revealed Himself to Israel as the Creator and the God of all nations and peoples. This is the truth that Israel was to proclaim to the nations. What a pity that Judaism came to look upon God as their own private deity, when the purpose for their existence as a distinct people was to reveal His goodness and truth to all people. Their selfishness and exclusiveness contradicted their primary affirmation about God. We must have clear views on the character of God. This lofty vision will shape lifestyle, relationships, attitudes, and behavior. Paul has good reason for focusing Timothy's attention on the "one God."

There is also "one Mediator between God and men" (vs. 5), Paul said. Notice that: one God and one Mediator. Mediation is one of Christianity's timeless, foundational truths. The one holy God can be approached only through a Mediator. He cannot countenance sin, and there is no human solution to the sin problem. That is the bad news. The good news is that Someone has been provided to "negotiate" the human predicament—"the man Christ Jesus, who gave himself a ransom for all men" (vss. 5, 6). There is no more profound concept in salvation history than that of the mediator. Angels could not possibly stand between God and the fallen race. The Mediator must be one who has the prerogatives of deity and the properties of humanity.

The Mediator provides a ransom (price of release) for all people (vs. 6). Sin involves penalties, costs, wages, payment. Jesus fully assumed humanity, with all of its liabilities, so that He could make payment on our behalf. "Our sins were laid on Christ, punished in Christ, put away by Christ" (*cited in Questions on Doctrine*, 672), is the way Ellen White puts it (see also Matt. 20:28; 1 Pet. 1:18, 19). Salvation is accomplished, the work of the Mediator is effective, general amnesty has been declared. Provision has been made for salvation from the penalty, power, and ultimately the very presence of sin. And all of this was done at the proper time, according to the divine schedule. "When the time had fully come, God sent his Son, born of a woman, born under law, to redeem those under law" (Gal. 4:4).

Paul the Herald

Paul now makes a sweeping declaration, toward which he has been moving: Incredible as it may sound, I have been appointed "a herald and an apostle" (vs. 7) of this message! Paul's tremendous sense that he had received a divine call comes through again and again in his letters. He continually makes a case for his authority. This is also evident in the pastoral epistles (see, for example, ch. 1:1). He has received this commission from none other than the Creator God—the God who will have all people to be saved.

He claims the offices of herald, apostle, and teacher. The herald brings an important announcement on behalf of his government or his superior. The proclamation of the message is basic. This creates the community of the saved. The community is sustained by the continued teaching of the message, the faith.

In the pastorals there is a special emphasis on a body of truths, the core teachings, that form the true faith. Paul brings us back to this time after time. His commission is to proclaim these truths to the Gentile world. As an envoy, he is a special representative of the King. As a witness, he puts his life on the line—willing to die the martyr's death, to make the supreme sacrifice, that the gospel might be proclaimed. The apostle is overwhelmed with his portfolio—God has made him an ambassador with full authority!

Men at Worship

Paul has strong opinions, and he states them with conviction. In this chapter he says, "I urge" (vs. 1), "I want" (vs. 8), "I also want" (vs. 9), and "I do not permit" (vs. 12). But his counsel at this point is for men only. He encourages "men everywhere to lift up holy hands in prayer, without anger or disputing" (vs. 8). Why is this so important? Because, as one modern author has said, "Where dissensions and disputings are engendered, earnest prayer is impeded. Prayer seeks the same tranquility for which the church prays with regards to civil authorities" (Oden, 92).

The Jews made a great matter of public piety. They could be seen regularly standing in the synagogues, in the temple court, or on the street corners, with their palms upturned, repeating their prayers. Jesus took note of this practice and commented on it (see Matt. 6:5; Mark 11:25; Acts 3:1). Worshipers bring a certain spirit to their worship. The Old Testament prophets thundered against men who brought their hard feelings and grudges to public worship. "Your fasting ends in quarreling and strife," Isaiah charged, "and in striking each other with wicked fists" (Isa. 58:4). Those who come to the service of worship are measured (see Rev. 11:1, KJV).

Women at Worship

The astounding thing here is that Paul does not exclude women from his counsel. He says, "I also want women" (vs. 9). He addresses women as responsible members of the community of faith. They are to be active participants in the worship service.

This was not the case in Judaism. Women were considered inferior and incapable of learning. No self-respecting rabbi would dare be seen conversing with a woman. Social mores and customs rigidly defined women's place. Along with the recitation of the *shema* (the confession of the one God), Jewish men prayed daily, "I thank Thee, O Lord, that I am not a Gentile, a slave, or a woman." The gospel writers, when reporting the number of people present at an event in Christ's ministry, followed the age-old practice of excluding women and children from the head count.

Thus it is revolutionary that Paul should give counsel to women in the same breath with his advice for men. This is a radical departure from the old norms. It is based on Paul's bold declaration in Galatians that "there is neither Jew nor Greek, slave nor free, male nor female, for you are all one in Christ Jesus" (Gal. 3:28).

Paul's departure from the culture of his time is all the more shocking when we consider that he is dealing with corporate worship. Freedom of worship for women and their equality with men was unthinkable in the synagogue. Christianity is indeed a clean break with the past. Theologians would call it a "discontinuity."

However, Paul does need to describe the new situation. How are women to react to the unqualified freedom that is now theirs in Christ? He begins with a recommendation that is concrete and practical: He wants women to dress modestly (vs. 9).

Much has been written about women's attire in the times of the apostles. A number of pagan writers decried the use of extravagant clothing that characterized certain classes of women. Extravagance and conspicuous consumption were the order of the day for those who could afford it. A common practice of the day was to weave gold and silver in the hair. Just as Paul considers praying with anger and doubt on the part of the men of the church to be inappropriate, so he considers it out of place for Christian women to dress for display or for sexual seduction.

It is important to note that Paul's advice on dress and adornment for women comes in the context of worship. Christian worship is addressed to the triune God. Paul warns all worshipers, both male and female, Beware of the attitude, the spirit, the motives, that you bring to worship!

Paul's counsel on dress is also in the context of "good deeds" (vs. 10). Fine deeds, character, adornment of the inner person, are highly desirable—far more than expensive clothes. The intelligent Christian woman adopts a lifestyle based on true values and spiritual realities. "For all of you who were baptized into Christ have clothed yourselves with Christ," Paul said in Galatians 3:27. This is "appropriate for women who profess to worship God" (vs. 10).

Paul is not just picking at women. In his view, women have a high and holy calling as members of the household of faith. Their deportment makes a statement to the world about the faith.

Not only does the apostle allow women status in worship, but he insists that "a woman should learn" (vs. 11). All the privileges of full church membership—hearing the word, joining in worship, involvement in fellowship, and participation in Christian service—are to be accessible to them (see Acts 1:14; 2:1-4, 42-47).

But the rule is that she learn "in quietness and full submission" (vs. 11). This newfound freedom must be exercised judiciously. Neither men nor women should give mixed signals about the faith to the larger community outside the church. False teachers (already mentioned in 1:1 and again in 2 Tim. 2) lead companies of silly, morally questionable women who are "always learning but never able to acknowledge the truth" (2 Tim. 3:7). Paul does not want true Christian women to be identified with this crowd. They must not be boisterous and pushy in the services. Already, pagan writers were charging Christians with being riff-raff, the uncultured scum of society. Heeding Paul's advice was the best way that Christian men and women could counter these allegations.

Paul extends his discussion of the quiet life to include the demeanor that women should exhibit in the assemblies. As the word is being taught, all of the worshipers are to be attentive. The apostle sees this as a feminine quality that adds to the quality of corporate worship. It is women's special gift to model the true spirit of worship.

What about submission? The apostle links the quiet spirit with submissiveness (vs. 11). Certainly Paul is not requiring that Christian women should be submissive to any and every male. In the household of faith, all are submissive to God, to church leaders (elders), and to each other. This submission does not mean inferiority. Christ was submissive to God, yet in every respect He was God, and "did not consider equality with God something to be grasped" (Phil. 2:6).

The Christian church is not to be a male-dominated patriarchy. It is the household of faith. God alone is Father, and we should call no man father (Matt. 23:9). The church is the place where all joyfully join together in worship. At the foot of the cross, the ground is level. There is to be order and system, and leadership is needed and recognized. But that leadership is always service-oriented (Matt. 20:25-27). Christians constitute a new kind of community. Every member of the household has equal dignity and standing.

Paul makes another point in this chapter that has created a great deal of discussion. "I do not permit a woman to teach," he says, "or to have authority over a man" (vs. 12). Apparently, the situation in Ephesus made this counsel necessary. Boisterous women (married or unmarried) must not usurp authority. Married women must not "boss" their husbands. Remember, the physical setting of the local congregation at that time was someone's home—often, no doubt, the home of one of the elders. There were probably a number of these cells of believers throughout Ephesus with "no more than fifteen to thirty members" (Beker, 319). That would be quite different from today's public worship setting! Everyone must respect the one who is teaching or prophesying. The rule of decency and order should be followed even in the informal worship of a house church.

The apostle also says that women must be silent. One cannot learn and talk at the same time. The counsel is good for men as well, but here it is directed to the women. Apparently some of them had contributed to disorder, and this was counterproductive to the mission of the church.

The apostle is here appealing to women as responsible members of the body of Christ. He does not promote male dominance. He does not encourage men to dominate women. This instruction is to the women. They are counseled to yield certain prerogatives for the gospel's sake on account of the present circumstances.

This is not the only place in his writings where Paul gave such advice. In 1 Corinthians 9:5-12 he pointed out that male apostles have the right both to marry and for their wives to accompany them on their travels. They also have a right to financial support from the churches for their labors. But Paul chose to surrender these prerogatives, these rights, for the sake of the gospel. So when Paul asks women to surrender a right, he is not backing away from Galatians 3:28, where he declares the basic principle of equality. He simply means that Christians should be willing to forego their rights for the sake of the gospel.

Going the second mile is the Christian posture. Jesus counseled His hearers to go beyond the injunction of law, as in the required Roman mile, and do the second mile of their own volition. An unscrupulous Roman in Christ's day might presumably have gotten a lot of free "baggage handling" by taking advantage of submissive Christians—asking first one and then another to carry his things an extra mile. However, Christ did not sanction the law that required even the first mile, and He certainly did not encourage the Romans to take advantage of their favored position. His advice was addressed to Christians, not to Romans. Similarly, Paul's advice in 1 Timothy 2 was addressed to women, not to men. This passage gives men no authority to dominate women.

Women by virtue of their baptism and the gift of God are fully accredited members of the community of faith. There are no second-class members in God's household. In the spirit of Christ, however, Paul is saying that Christian women should be willing to forego some of their prerogatives so that the missionary purpose of the church may be enhanced. The church today, however, must not codify the temporary injunction into law. We must live in the hope and work toward the end that circumstances will change and that the Spirit of God will, in time, show us "a better way."

Theodoret explained the counsel on silence in the assembly in this way: "Since women too have the benefit of the prophetic gift, it was necessary that he give instructions about that" (Dibelius, 48). That Paul never intended women to always be silent in church is evident from his advice to the church at Corinth, in which he said that "every woman who prays or prophesies with her head uncovered dishonors her head" (1 Cor. 11:5). Apparently it was a custom of the time for women to keep their heads covered in church. The point is that Paul *did* allow women to speak in church. Thus his advice in 1 Timothy 2:12 for a woman to be silent in church should be understood as applicable to a particular situation in the church at Ephesus at the time Paul wrote his epistle, and not as a rule for all women at all times.

Overly assertive women need to be reminded that it was Eve's insistence on independence that led to her deception, "for Adam was formed first, then Eve" (vs. 13). The apostle is not setting up a "pecking order," nor is he attaching all blame for the fall to Eve. While it is true that Eve should have stayed by the side of her companion, there is enough blame to go around.

The Bible is not interested in promoting male or female dominance. The Scriptures are clear that it takes both male and female to constitute humanity. Complementariness, mutual support, and submission to the other are what is required, both in the church and in marriage. "In the Lord, however, woman is not independent of man, nor is man independent of woman. For as woman came from man, so also man is born of woman. But everything comes from God" (1 Cor. 11:11, 12).

What does Paul mean at the conclusion of chapter 2 when he says, "Women will be kept safe through childbirth" (vs. 15)? Notice that he does not say a woman is saved *by* childbearing, because salvation is all of grace. Nor does he mean that Christian women are guaranteed that they will not die in giving birth. Many godly women have died during the birth experience.

Paul is saying that although women do experience birth pains, (the man was sentenced to eat bread by the sweat of his face), this "curse" need not threaten their salvation, "if they continue in faith, love and holiness with propriety" (vs. 15). These are the qualities that identify all those who are being saved, both men and women. Women are also recipients of God's saving grace, and no condition imposed on them can change this. Their destiny is not cast by the historical account. It is true that the woman was first in transgression, but this does not negate the provision made for her salvation. There is somewhat of a divine irony here. The Christ Child is the seed of the woman! (Gen. 3:15; Gal. 4:4; Rev. 12:1, 2). The counsel is intended to encourage and affirm the women of the church.

Note on Chapter 2:11-15

The church is the community where the will of God is done on earth "as it is in heaven." The principles of the kingdom of God are to be demonstrated here. It is the ideal community. It is God's household. All members of the family have equal status before God and are responsible and accountable for service and ministry. All are recipients of the gifts, and all are expected to share what they have received in order that the fellowship be built up. The church is duty bound to recognize and make room for the exercise of the gifts.

The question of ordination is not central to the agenda in the pastoral epistles. Service and leadership and church order are primary in the apostle's mind. The present-day church must take care that its theology of ordination is not an import from the apostasy. Roman Catholicism is essentially a sacerdotal religion. At its foundation, sacerdotalism is power invested in an earthly priesthood. Ordination was never intended to confer special "irrevocable and indelible" powers to human beings.

Ministry and leadership under the new covenant are no longer determined by tribe or gender. Both Jesus and Paul ignored man-made restrictions imposed on people. Jesus shocked the religious establishment of His day when He spoke to women in public. He included them in the band of disciples who assisted Him in ministry, and He included them in the great commission.

Paul included women as colleagues in ministry. Priscilla was recognized as a teacher—the apostle did not think it out of place for her to instruct Apollos (Acts 18:26). He speaks with deep appreciation for "these women who have contended at my side in the cause of the gospel" (Phil. 4:3). In the famous greeting list of Romans 16, women are mentioned side by side with their male counterparts without the slightest inference of inequality (Rom. 16:1-15). He calls Phoebe a deacon, and he does not use the female *deaconess*. Junia is numbered among the apostles.

Seventh-day Adventists who wish to use Scripture to limit the Spirit's prerogative to give gifts for ministry without reference to gender are hard put to explain the ministry of Ellen White. Was it of God or of men? Was it a temporary suspension of the rules, or was it a fulfillment of Joel's prophecy (Joel 2:28-32), a breakthrough toward the full empowerment of all God's people? The New Testament emphasizes the gifts of the Spirit for all members, given for building up the entire fellowship of believers.

■ Applying the Word

1. **On what grounds can Christians pray for dishonest political leaders who abuse their office for personal gain? On what grounds can they pray for dictators and leaders of totalitarian states who allow political dissidents to be tortured? Peter refused to obey the government in Jerusalem (see Acts 4:19, 20). How can we know where**

to draw the line between obedience to the government and obedience to God?

2. Paul seems to place a high premium on godliness (vs. 2). Look up parallel passages on the godly life in the pastorals and other New Testament references (1 Tim. 4:8; 6:11; Titus 1:1; 2 Pet. 1:3; 1:6, 7; 3:11). How can this be worked out in terms of living in the nineties? What is the meaning of practical godliness? Put a modern face on it.

3. How can I apply Paul's advice about Christian grooming and dress to my own time? Should Christian women avoid going to the beauty parlor? What principle underlies his advice about the use of jewelry? Does this same principle apply to neckties worn by men? How can a Christian know what constitutes costly clothing? How can I apply Paul's admonition to dress modestly (vss. 9, 10)? What is the best way to make this counsel relevant and an aid to Christian growth in the nineties?

4. How does Paul's admonition to men at prayer (vs. 8) apply to my church and to local congregations generally today? How does his counsel to the women at Ephesus (vs. 9) apply to congregations today? What attitudes, feelings, and prejudices do we bring to the service of worship that impede our prayers?

■ Researching the Word

1. Use a concordance to look up all the New Testament references to prayer (including the words *pray, prayed, prayers,* and *praying*). Make a note of each one that suggests an attitude with which Christians should pray. From this study, what conclusions can you draw about the effect that our attitude in prayer has on the effectiveness of our prayers? What lessons do you learn from this study that can improve your own attitudes in prayer?

2. Look up in a concordance all the references listed under "woman" and "women" in the Gospels. From this study, what conclusions can you draw about Jesus' atti-

tude toward women and the relationship that He had
with women? Read the long article under the word
women in the *Seventh-day Adventist Bible Dictionary*.
What changes in the status of women in society came
about as a result of the ministry of both Jesus and Paul?
How do Paul's remarks about women in 1 Timothy 2 fit
into this overall picture?

∎ Further Study of the Word

1. For more information on the role of women in the
   church, see "Theology of Women," *A Woman's Place*,
   Rosa Taylor Banks, ed., 13-40; Ellen G. White, *Welfare
   Ministry*, 143-166; *Evangelism*, 471-474, 491-493.
2. On mediation, see Charles E. Bradford, *The God Between*,
   43-53.
3. On Christ as Mediator, see Francis D. Nichol, ed.,
   Seventh-day Adventist Bible Commentary, 8:722, 723.
4. On ordination, see V. Norskov Olsen, "Ordination,"
   Myth and Truth: Church, Priesthood and Ordination,
   119-128, 140-149; on the priesthood of believers, see
   39-46.
5. On the Christian's dress, see *Seventh-day Adventists Believe . . .* , 286, 287.

CHAPTER THREE

Counsels on the Well-ordered Community

1 Timothy 3

Paul has been approaching his task methodically. He has set forth the reason and urgency for his letter. His instruction to Timothy is, stop the false teachers and their destructive activities. The apostle then proceeds to profile the false teachers and to point out the nature and the deplorable result of their teachings. In chapter 2 he urges upon the church the ministry of prayer in the broadest and most inclusive terms. Now he comes to the crux of the matter: how the church is to be ordered and structured so that it may do its saving work in the world and so that its members may grow up into the stature of Christ, men and women who are perfect in unity and love.

The church is preserved and protected by its doctrines, its belief system. It is also guarded by its organization and structure. Early Seventh-day Adventists called this structuring of the church "gospel order." The church—a praying, worshiping community—must also be an ordered community. "Everything should be done in a fitting and orderly way" (1 Cor. 14:40). Even redeemed humanity, brought together as the community of those who are being saved, needs an organizing principle. If the body of Christ is to fulfill its missionary purpose, it must be structured.

Organization gives shape and form to the body so that there will be no division. The body is designed for function, for service. And that body needs ministries and a variety of ministering servants (officers) to see to it that its functions are carried out harmoniously and that the body serves its members and the world effectively. Only in this way can the church fulfill the purpose for which Christ established it.

59

■ Getting Into the Word

Read chapter 3 several times. Read it again in every Bible version available to you. Then respond to the following questions:

1. Notice the various ways the Greek word *episcopos* (overseer) is translated in the different versions. Do you think this church leader is a local elder, or is he in charge of a district or diocese of churches?

2. Acts 6:1-6 tells about the appointment of seven men to care for food distribution. What occasioned this advanced step in church organization (Acts 6:1, 2)? Who made the selection of the new officers (vs. 5)? What was the congregation's part in the matter (vs. 6)? What did the apostles do then? Was this another layer of bureaucracy, or was it a wise use of talent in the church (vs. 7)?

3. Christianity has its roots in Judaism. For an overview of how leadership functioned in Old Testament times, review the following passages: Numbers 11:16-27; Exodus 18:13-23; 2 Samuel 3:17; 5:3; 1 Kings 8:1-3; 12:6-8; Ezra 10:8. Reflect on these Old Testament patterns of leadership as you go through chapter 3. To what extent were the emerging New Testament patterns of leadership influenced by the Old Testament account? From your reading of verses 1 to 7, make a list of spiritual qualities and character traits for local elders. How do the requirements for the deacons compare with those for elders? What meaning does this have for the church today?

4. Verse 11 reviews the spiritual qualifications of deacons' wives. (The Greek allows it to be translated "women," as in the RSV.) Could this refer to deaconesses? Why are elders' wives not mentioned? Why do you think Paul begins verse 11 with the phrase "in the same way"? What title did Paul give Phoebe in Romans 16:1?

5. How does verse 15 indicate that all the people of God are responsible for sustaining the mission of the church? How does this relate to Exodus 19:3-6 and 1 Peter 2:9,

10, where the people of God are referred to as priests?
What are the implications in this concept for the role
and function of laypersons in today's church?

■ Exploring the Word

Church Offices and Officers

The phrase "Here is a trustworthy saying" (vs. 1) is Paul's way
of flagging an important passage. Some manuscripts place it at
the end of chapter 1. The phrase is translated variously as "true
saying," "a saying you can rely on," "the Christian message meant
to be believed," "stands firm," "a popular saying," and "is true
and irrefutable." However we translate it, the clause forms a bridge
or transition between the opening section of the letter and all that
follows.

The office or work of overseer is considered to be a "noble
task" (vs. 1). The emphasis here is on the service rather than the
position. In Paul's view, to aspire to this kind of noble service is
legitimate. Persons with gifts of leadership are to be encouraged
to develop their gifts.

The word translated as *overseer* (vs. 2) in the NIV is in some
other versions rendered elder, bishop, presiding officer, president,
superintendent, or pastor. The terms are interchangeable. (This
is not a new position. See Acts 11:30; 14:23; 20:17, 28.)

The term *elder* probably says it best. In every ancient society
and in some modern ones as well, the most respected and best
recognized religious and civic leaders are called elders. This was
true in the Greek city states, in Roman social and political organizations, and especially in Judaism. The term *city fathers* is still used.
The word *alderman* stems from *elder*. If there is a universal or
natural ordering of society, it seems to be based on the idea that
wisdom and authority reside in a council of elders and that they
should be given status and authority.

Paul's idea of organization is not hard to understand. His rec-
ommendations are practical and understandable, even in a pagan
society. Romans, Jews, and Greeks developed their moral codes.
Ancient philosophers talked about virtue. The people wanted to
feel that their leaders had character, integrity. Could Christians

expect anything less of their leaders? Paul knew that the cause of Christ would be judged by its leadership. The list of qualifications was in some ways familiar to the people of the day.

The elder. First, there is the elder/overseer (vss. 1-7). What kind of person should the leader of a community of Christians be? He should be "above reproach" (vs. 2). He should not be a lightning rod for scandal. This is devastating to the fellowship. The church must insist on and maintain high standards for its elders. Is this unreasonable? Paul does not think so. If the church does not examine its leaders prior to their appointment, the world will certainly do so after they have been placed in office. Elders accept their assignments voluntarily. They are not to be forced into office. In the early church, leadership often involved risk and personal danger. The leaders of the church were the first to feel the sting of persecution. As the leader of his household, the elder was held responsible for the conduct or misconduct of its members.

Some historians say that polygamy was a greater problem among Jews than among pagans in the first century. It is no wonder that the apostle required a monogamous lifestyle of the church's spiritual leaders. There is no hesitation here! Leadership in Christ's church must be different from that of the synagogue or the pagan temple. The elder must be the husband of one wife. Does this mean that only married men qualify? If this were the meaning of Paul's counsel, then Paul himself would not have met the criteria! Does this mean that he must not be a remarried person, even if he were at one time a widower? The question must be answered in the context of the New Testament teaching on marriage. Paul is not making canon law. His counsel is simple and straightforward: elders should be of impeccable character in every respect. An adulterous, promiscuous lifestyle is absolutely incompatible with the calling of an elder.

The elder should be "temperate, self-controlled, respectable, [and] hospitable" (vs. 2). He should have teaching and communication skills (vs. 2). Paul also mentions some negatives: "Not given to much wine, not violent but gentle, not quarrelsome, not a lover of money" (vs. 3). The good sense of these qualifications is self-evident.

Verse 4 deals with the elder's management strengths, beginning with his own family. We must remember that the churches were at that time meeting in private homes, and some of the elders were probably heads of these households. The leadership of an elder who could not command the respect of his own children would be seriously impaired.

Yet another qualification is mentioned: "He must not be a recent convert" (literally, "newly planted"). And the reason is clear: "Or he may become conceited and fall under the same judgment as the devil" (vs. 6). Elders were highly regarded and esteemed. Authority is difficult for even the most seasoned person to carry with balance and grace. The stability of the congregation depends to a great degree upon the equilibrium and trustworthiness of its leader. Pride and conceit placed Lucifer under severe judgment.

Once again the apostle has his eye on the community that is to be evangelized, for he says that the elder "must also have a good reputation with outsiders, so that he will not fall into disgrace and into the devil's trap" (vs. 7). Notice that the elders are Satan's special target. Satan uses pride and deceit and love of power as his snare. During the latter part of the 1980s, a number of prominent Christian leaders in America were caught misusing funds and engaging in adulterous relationships. The scandal that resulted brought disgrace on all Christian churches.

Paul has little to say here about the skills of the elder. Only two items fall into the category of a job description: The ability to teach (vs. 2) and management/people skills (vss. 4, 5). The emphasis is more on the character qualifications that the spiritual leader should possess. The apostle could not have made the case more clearly.

The deacon. The word *deacon* is translated from the Greek *diakonos*, which means "servant." In some instances it is rendered "helper." In a sense this is applicable to all Christians, including apostles. Christ spoke of Himself as a servant. The leaders in God's household are servants, not rulers.

The qualifications for deacons are similar to those for elders. "Deacons, likewise, are to be men worthy of respect" (vs. 8). The emphasis is on lifestyle. They are to be temperate, sincere, and honest. One would expect that an elder should be sound in doctrine, but Paul points out that deacons must also have clear doctrinal views and a good grasp on the fundamentals of the faith (vs. 9). Office holders must have deep convictions, and they should be able to set them forth clearly so that they can defend the faith.

Deacons should be examined and tested before their appointment to office. A period of internship or probation is in order. The whole church is involved in the selection process. "If there is nothing against them, let them serve as deacons" (vs. 10).

Wives or deaconesses? Verse 11 can refer to deacons' wives or to deaconesses (see the NIV margin on vs. 11; see also the marginal explanation in the RSV). Phoebe (Romans 16:1) was called a deaconess (servant) of the church. I take the position that the reference in Paul's letter to Timothy is to female deacons, what we today call deaconesses. If the reference were to wives, we would expect to find a corresponding treatment of elders' wives in verses 1 to 7. But that is not the case. Elders' wives are not even mentioned.

Paul's use of the phrase "in the same way" (vs. 11) may be a clue. He seems to be addressing three groups of church leaders: (1) The elder "must be . . ."; (2) "Deacons, likewise, are to be . . ."; and (3) "In the same way" female deacons "are to be . . ." Spouses are not addressed in the series. The list that follows for the women is a shortened version of the qualifications for deacons and elders. Female helpers should be "worthy of respect, not malicious talkers but temperate and trustworthy in everything" (vs. 11).

Verse 12 addresses the marital status of the deacon and his ability to manage his house well. Verse 13 refers not only to deacons but to elders and female leaders as well. This ties in to verse 1— service in the house of God is a noble task, and though difficult and demanding, it is also rewarding. All who serve faithfully will grow in usefulness and in the respect of the people, believers and nonbelievers.

Offices are for the purpose of serving the church, and they emerge from the church's needs (see Acts 6:1-6). By the time Paul wrote to Timothy, two offices, elders and deacons, seem to have developed.

It is instructive to note how the New Testament uses the word *diakonos.* Service is the central idea. Jesus and the apostles refer to themselves as servants and to their work as service. Ministry is service. The gifts of the Spirit are spoken of as service. It is striking how the whole New Testament is permeated with the concept of the church as servant, patterned after the selfless service of Jesus, who was the Servant of all. It bears repeating, therefore, that offices in the church are for service, not rulership. Position is always an opportunity for service. The greater the position, the greater the service that is required. The Holy Spirit chose a word that has as its origin the idea of "table service" and made it the vehicle to convey the kind of leadership that is acceptable in the church.

Conduct in God's Household

In Paul's day, writing a letter was the next best thing to being there, just as in our day telephoning would be next best. Yet even at its very best, correspondence is a distant second to talking face to face. The apostle says he is hoping to be physically present for fellowship with the Ephesian believers in the near future, but he has instruction that he is anxious for Timothy to receive as soon as possible. He wrote out the instructions (1 Timothy) and "mailed" them on the chance that he might be delayed. It was probably just as well that he did this, because we have no record of Paul visiting Ephesus after he wrote this letter.

The crux of the matter is behavior, interpersonal relationships, life in the community of faith, God's household (the church)— "how people ought to conduct themselves" (vs. 15) in this fellowship. How does the Christian faith come to expression in the home, the church as it gathers for worship, and the marketplace? In other words, where is the church on Monday morning? God has high expectations for His people. Great privileges call for corresponding responsibility. He wants to make every member "a pillar in the temple" (Rev. 3:12). The church is "the pillar and foundation of the truth" (vs. 15). Its members are called living stones, and are, as Ellen White says, to be "emitting light" (*Christian Service*, 62). We are accountable for the light we have received. The world is convinced not so much by the church's pronouncements as by the way it lives those proclaimed truths. This is how the church becomes the pillar and foundation of the truth.

The Mystery of Godliness

"Beyond all question, the mystery of godliness is great" (vs. 16). After an extended discussion of serious issues and theological concepts, Paul sometimes breaks forth in a hymn of thanksgiving or a litany of praise. The Scriptures speak of two great mysteries: the mystery of godliness and the mystery of iniquity. Mystery in this sense is not some riddle or puzzle, but a deep spiritual truth that can be understood only through the assistance of the Holy Spirit.

Briefly stated, and somewhat oversimplified, the mystery of iniquity is a creature assuming the prerogatives of Deity, such as Lucifer attempting to raise his throne above the stars of God and be "like the Most High" (Isaiah 14:12-14). The culmination of this arrogance is "the man of lawlessness . . . [who] opposes and exalts himself over everything that is called God or is worshiped, and even sets himself in God's temple, proclaiming himself to be God" (2 Thessalonians 2:3, 4).

The mystery of godliness, simply put, is God giving up the prerogatives of Deity and becoming a man. There is no greater or more profound spiritual truth. This is the theme of a great hymn (Philippians 2:6-11). Paul is always overcome with awe and gratitude at the mention of the incarnation. Plain prose will not do. He must take the wings of poetic flight and sanctified imagination. This is indeed rarified atmosphere.

A Closing Hymn

The early Christians sang "psalms, hymns and spiritual songs" (Col. 3:16). The words or lyrics of these songs were carefully chosen for their teaching value. As they sang the words, the truths of the gospel were fastened in people's minds. The pious Jews had followed this practice for centuries. Jesus sang the psalms. This was a time-honored teaching device.

Verse 16 constitutes one of these carefully crafted hymns. Paul probably did not write it, but rather quoted a hymn that was well known among the believers at the time. The subject is Christ incarnate, risen, and ascended. It speaks of His resurrection and ascension in the power of the Spirit, and of His installation at the right hand of God, when He sent His Spirit to be the chief administrator of the church. Father, Son, and Holy Spirit work together in perfect unity for our salvation. There is no interruption in the divine administration.

The New International Version divides the poem into three stanzas, each with two lines. The first line, "He appeared in a body," presents Christ in His incarnation, God made visible, manifest in human form.

The second line lifts up the risen Lord: He "was vindicated by the Spirit." The King James Version says, "Justified in the Spirit." However, the NIV use of the word *vindicated* is probably closer to what the early Christian community understood, since Jesus certainly did not need justification for salvation as sinful human beings do. The mission of the Holy Spirit is to glorify Jesus. In Romans Paul wrote, "Who through the Spirit of holiness was declared with power to be the Son of God by his resurrection from the dead" (Rom. 1:4). These two lines remind us that in His incarnation Christ did not cease to be the divine Son of God.

Paul's statement that the resurrected Jesus "was seen by angels" would surely refer to the angel who called Him forth from the grave and the angels who remained behind to inform the disciples of His resurrection. However, it probably refers even more appropriately to the welcome the angels must surely have given to Jesus upon His triumphant return to heaven to take up His ministry in the heavenly sanctuary as our High Priest.

Next, Paul says that Jesus "was preached among the nations." Jesus commanded His disciples to make disciples of all nations (Matt. 28:19). This is the work of the church. Embedding it in a hymn kept the early church's mission ever before the members' eyes.

Continuing the theme of gospel proclamation, the hymn points to the success of the gospel commission: Jesus "was believed on in the world." Christ continues His existence in the church—the fellowship of believers.

The hymn concludes with the words, He "was taken up in glory." Again we are reminded of Christ's ascension, which marks the beginning of the age of the Spirit.

■ Applying the Word

1. As members of the body of Christ, we have an obligation to learn as much as we can about how our church functions. Review the roster of your local church's officers. How many elders, deacons, and deaconesses are listed? How are they organized? Find out how often your church board meets. What items does the usual church board agenda cover? In what ways can you be more supportive of your local church leaders? What is the local conference's responsibility in enhancing the ministry of local church leaders? Pray for your church officers, and ask God what you can do to facilitate their work.

2. If you hold an office in your church, what instruction does Paul give in 1 Timothy 3 that can help you to be more effective in carrying it out? To what extent do you meet his character qualifications for the offices of elder, deacon, and deaconess? Where can you improve? What might you do today that would be a step toward improvement?

3. Why are the words to hymns so important? What is the teaching value of the lyrics? What could be the possible effects of singing hymns that contain theological error? How can you make the words to hymns more meaningful as you sing? What programs might your church put in place to help members better understand the importance of the above concepts?

4. The great hymn of verse 16 extols the incarnation of Christ. How does the incarnation work out in practical terms in your own experience? In the family unit? In the life of the church? How does Philippians 2:5-8 deepen the appeal of the hymn?

■ Researching the Word

1. Read the guidelines for the offices of elder, deacon, and deaconess as given in the *Seventh-day Adventist Church Manual*, preferably the most recent edition (available from your Adventist Book Center if you do not own a

copy). Look up all the Bible passages listed. Do you find qualifications or aspects of job descriptions in the manual that go beyond what is given in the Bible? If so, do you feel that these qualifications and details of job descriptions are appropriate in spite of the lack of biblical support? What is the basis for your conclusion (e. g.: Ellen White's writings, common sense, etc.)? Do you find qualifications or aspects of job descriptions mentioned in the Bible that are not included in the *Church Manual*'s guidelines that perhaps should be added?

2. Read the article titled "Mystery" in the *Seventh-day Adventist Bible Dictionary*. Use a concordance to look up all the occurrences of the word *mystery* in the New Testament. Make a list of all the things that are called "mysteries." What deep spiritual truth makes each one a mystery? What lesson that is helpful to your spiritual life can you gain from understanding each of these mysteries? Does any one theme run through all of these mysteries that unites them under a single principle or truth? After completing this study, write your own definition of the word *mystery* as it is used in the New Testament.

■ Further Study of the Word

1. For an understanding of the principles on which Seventh-day Adventist church government is based, see *Seventh-day Adventists Believe . . .* , 145-148.

2. For information about church officers and their duties, see *Seventh-day Adventist Church Manual*, 1981 edition, "Church Officers and Their Duties," 53-65.

3. For additional information about the biblical qualifications and job descriptions of elders, deacons, and deaconesses, look up these words in Siegfried H. Horn, et. al., *Seventh-day Adventist Bible Dictionary*; *Harper's Bible Dictionary*, s.v. "ministry," 168, 254.

4. For a better understanding of ordination, see V. Norskov Olsen, "The Nature of Ministry," in *Myth and Truth—Church, Priesthood and Ordination*.

CHAPTER FOUR

General Counsels

1 Timothy 4

Chapter 3 ends with a hymn extolling the great mystery of godliness—Christ in human flesh working out the salvation of the world. The hymn introduces the ministry of the Holy Spirit, who vindicates Christ's mission and superintends the work of salvation (the continuance of the mystery of God) during the time between His ascension and His second coming.

To open chapter 4, Paul revisits the issues and concerns that prompted the writing of his letter; namely, the false teachers and their teaching. Chapter 4 is the most systematic treatment of false teachers in the pastoral epistles. He calls attention to the Holy Spirit, who guides the church and its individual believers. He points out dangers and pitfalls. Thus Satan's strategies come as no surprise to the Christian who hears what the Spirit has to say. The relevant word from the Spirit is, There is apostasy on the horizon. "Wherever truth flourishes error raises its ugly head" (Guthrie, 103).

The apostle also has some fitting words of admonition for his son Timothy in face of the coming crisis. Timothy must give attention to his own person, spiritual fitness, and leadership style—the essentials of his teaching and preaching ministry. Both his salvation and that of his hearers depend on the faithful discharge of his ministerial duties.

■ Getting Into the Word

Read 1 Timothy 4 through two times. Then work on the following items. If you are keeping a notebook, write down your answers to the questions:

70

1. In the context of 4:1-5, what does Paul mean by "later times" in verse 1? Do you think the phrase is more closely related to 2 Timothy 3:1 or to Acts 20:29-31? Why?

2. With the aid of a concordance, study the New Testament's use of the word *conscience*. List the conclusions you can draw from your study. What is the problem with the consciences of 4:2? How does the work of the Holy Spirit relate to one's conscience? What relationship, if any, do you find between Matthew 12:31, 32 and the conscience problems in 1 Timothy 4:2? Consult a Bible dictionary on the word *conscience*, and compare your findings.

3. Make a list of the problems Paul is describing in 4:1-5. Within the context of 1 Timothy, write a sentence or two describing the significance of each item in your list.

4. In 4:6-16 Paul describes the characteristics of the good minister. List those characteristics. Why is each important?

■ Exploring the Word

The Approaching Apostasy

The New Testament era is the age of the Spirit. The Holy Spirit is the chief administrator of the mission of God. Jesus promised that "he will tell you what is yet to come" (John 16:13). Paul does not point to a specific prophecy but says, "The Spirit clearly says that in later times some will abandon the faith and follow deceiving spirits and things taught by demons" (ch. 4:1). Prophetic guidance is the heritage of those who are loyal to Jesus. The Ephesian church, however, must have known about this prophecy. Paul referred to his own ministry in Ephesus as preaching "anything that would be helpful to you" (Acts 20:20). One of these helpful words of warning was about the "savage wolves [that] will come in among you and will not spare the flock" (Acts 20:29).

The New Testament records instances when the Holy Spirit spoke through contemporary prophets to warn the church about imminent dangers. Twice the prophet Agabus was moved by the

Holy Spirit to give such prophetic warnings (Acts 11:28; 21:10). In fact, the mission of the apostolic church is so directly supervised by the Holy Spirit that the book of Acts is more like the acts of the Holy Spirit than it is the acts of the apostles.

"Later times" here does not refer exclusively to the last days of earth's history. Paul means sometime in the future, "after I leave" (Acts 20:29). During these later times—the days ahead—there will be casualties, defections from the faith, dropouts. In the fierce struggle, "some will abandon the faith and follow deceiving spirits and things taught by demons" (vs. 1). There will be an upsurge in demonic activity. Of course, this will be seen again with greater intensity in the final days of earth's history.

Paul's statement that "some will abandon the faith" is evidence contradicting the teaching that born-again Christians can never fall from grace (the popular saying is "once saved, always saved" or "once in Christ, never out"). There is no such thing as an irrevocable, eternal life insurance policy. God will never revoke it, but we can. Believers are in a struggle against "the powers" (Eph. 6:12). It is warfare, and war has its casualties. The church needs to know the enemy and the nature of the conflict.

The false teachers are mere pawns of demonic forces. Their consciences are seared "as with a hot iron" (vs. 2). Paul uses the medical term *cauterized*. The Ephesian heretics have become agents of evil angels, and they do their bidding. They have sold out to the enemy.

What is the nature of their apostasy? "They forbid people to marry and order them to abstain from certain foods, which God created to be received with thanksgiving by those who believe and who know the truth" (vs. 3). Why is this so disturbing to the apostle? Because it is basically an attack on God's good creation and a misrepresentation of the Creator's intent and plan. Marriage and foods are both gifts of God to the human family for their enjoyment and have been pronounced good. But as with all God's gifts, there are parameters and a context within which they are to be enjoyed. It has always been Satan's strategy to misconstrue and demean God's plan. The heretics, Paul warned, would pervert the gifts of God through a false self-denial.

In his first letter to Timothy, Paul provides us with one of the earliest references to a heresy that gained tremendous influence for several centuries thereafter and caused serious conflicts in Christendom. This false theological system came to be known as Gnosticism, from the Greek word *gnosis*, which means "knowledge." In 1 Timothy 6:20 Paul uses the word *gnosis* in a derogatory sense—what is "falsely called knowledge." The name *Gnosticism* as applied to this false system derives from the fact that the Gnostics claimed to have special insight or knowledge. Paul warns Timothy to keep away from this mishmash of Greek philosophy and Jewish speculation.

The Gnostics taught that physical matter was evil and that it was not created by the good God but by an evil deity. They rejected the body as being corrupt from creation to the present, and they extolled the spirit or soul as being superior and untainted by the flawed creation. They felt that marriage was of the flesh and quite beneath the high spiritual state of those who had embraced such lofty views. The Gnostics believed that salvation comes through a special knowledge that only the initiated receive. Good and evil were explained by the introduction of several deities, one of which was responsible for evil. The God of Israel and His Christ were assigned minor roles in the scheme of things.

We do not know when this seductive system of error came to full flower in the Christian church, but we see it in its early stages of development in Colossae, probably in Corinth, and certainly in Ephesus, as is evident in Paul's first letter to Timothy. In his letter to the Christians at Colossae, Paul said, "See to it that no one takes you captive through hollow and deceptive philosophy, which depends on human tradition and the basic principles of this world rather than on Christ" (Col. 2:8). Paul uses *philosophia* to indicate Jewish sophistry. His remarks to the Corinthians help us to understand a bit more about the nature of this heresy: "Jews demand miraculous signs and Greeks look for wisdom" (1 Cor. 1:22). For centuries, Jews had been imbibing Greek thought and culture and attempting to integrate these sentiments into Judaism. Now some Christians were following suit.

This mixture of the mystical elements of Hebrew and Greek thought made an intoxicating brew. Pseudointellectuals were fascinated by its high-sounding sentiments. It also appealed to human pride. There was no cross involved in accepting its teachings. Gnosticism in all forms and at all stages of development promised escape from the demanding obligations and the tough realities of life. One could reach a higher plane of existence and freedom in the mastery of the secret knowledge and wisdom of the sages. Ordinary work, especially manual labor, was looked down on as beneath the station of one who had been initiated into the *gnosis*—superior knowledge.

However, there is danger in reading too much into 1 Timothy. If we say that Paul was responding to the full-blown manifestation of gnosticism, then we are placing the time of the pastoral epistles at least 100 years after the days of the apostles. This is the position of scholars who assign authorship to someone other than Paul. We hold the position that the pastorals are without question Pauline and were written during the A.D. 60s.

Heresies About Marriage

One of the heresies of these false teachers was that they forbade their followers to marry. Paul saw in this teaching the seeds of a future heresy that would carry many away from the truth. Such teaching is diametrically opposed to the true doctrine of creation, in which a perfect God created matter that He called good and instituted marriage as a great blessing to humanity. "God saw all that he had made, and it was very good" (Gen. 1:31). "He who finds a wife finds what is good and receives favor from the Lord" (Prov. 18:22; see also Gen. 2:18, 24; Heb. 13:4).

The God of the Bible provides food and material blessings as a part of His covenant with the human family (Ps. 103:5; 104:14; Heb. 8:10, 12; Isa. 55:2). The Bible knows nothing of a lesser god who is responsible for the material world. It knows only of Yahweh, whose very name suggests that He is sole Creator—the One who causes all things to be.

Food Taboos

Along with their heretical teachings on marriage, the false teachers "order them [church members in Ephesus] to abstain from certain foods" (vs. 3). Their reasoning was that food was a necessary evil, and the "enlightened" should avoid partaking of certain foods that were deemed more soul defiling than others. It should be kept in mind that the false teachers were smooth operators who made an impressive show of religiosity. They had an air of holiness about them that made it difficult to oppose them. We can imagine how they looked down on the youthful Timothy as intellectually inferior to themselves and thus incapable of seriously challenging their superior brand of knowledge.

Paul uses the argument of the good creation to refute the heretics. "Everything God created is good, and nothing is to be rejected if it is received with thanksgiving" (vs. 4). Was Paul pleading for the abandonment of the principles of diet that had been a blessing to Israel for millenniums? Certainly not!

The key to understanding this passage is the clause "because it is consecrated by the word of God and prayer" (vs. 5). The Word had pronounced certain foods as good for human consumption from Creation (Genesis 1:29; 3:18; 8:20). There was no quarrel in the early church about eating foods declared unclean by Scripture. The problem in Corinth was food offered to idols (1 Cor. 8), and before that, eating with unwashed hands (Matt. 15:17-20). It was a question of ceremonial, ritual purity. The false teachers' theories were "but rules taught by men" (Matt. 15:9). The Jerusalem council addressed the problem of food candidly (Acts 15:20, 29). It should be pointed out that the cross made no physical change in human beings or animals. What the cross did for believing Gentiles was to purify "their hearts by faith" (Acts 15:9). Peter gave an inspired interpretation of his vision of a sheet let down from heaven containing "all kinds of four-footed animals, as well as reptiles" (Acts 10:12). He said, "God has shown me that I should not call any man impure or unclean" (vs. 28). Paul's counsel to Timothy had to do with the food restrictions of the Gnostics of his day, not with Jewish food restrictions.

The foundation of every man-made religion is the attempt to gain merit toward salvation through human effort. It was not the Holy Spirit that actuated the false teachers' prohibitions but their desire to establish their own righteousness apart from Christ. The gifts of God to His children are to be received with a prayer of thanksgiving (vs. 5).

The wise man's counsel is, "Do not be overrighteous, neither be overwise" (Ecc. 7:16). The Anchor Bible translates this verse, "Do not be overscrupulous, or make a fetish of wisdom." This is precisely what the false teachers at Ephesus were doing. This made them haughty, overbearing, arrogant, and authoritarian. They felt quite competent to prescribe for others, even to commanding people to conform to their beliefs and practices.

On the other hand, the obedient, thankful child of God is full of gratitude for all God's marvelous gifts. He is not indifferent about diet and health. God's faithful people live by the New Testament injunction, "Whether you eat or drink or whatever you do, do it all for the glory of God" (1 Cor. 10:31). Christians are sober and self-denying, but never overly so.

Further Profiling of the False Teachers

The false teachers are pretenders, playactors—hypocrites (vs. 2). They claim to have found a higher revelation of truth than others. Further, they declare that they are the true church and that they are the real defenders of the faith. In Seventh-day Adventist parlance, they profess to have "new light." Their act is so persuasive that people are carried away in the deception because it appeals to their pride. "There is nothing which looks better than hypocrisy," says Luther. "It carries the title of God, Christ, righteousness, truth, church. It has the applause of the whole world. . . . Hypocrisy is the effectiveness of error. . . . It is the nature of all hypocrites and false prophets to create a conscience where there is none, and to cause conscience to disappear where it does exist" (quoted in Oden, 59).

Sensitive people who have overworked consciences are an easy prey for these religious charlatans. False teachers take delight in exercising a kind of thought control. Their own seared consciences give them a fascinating pleasure in this power. At the same time, these religious fanatics are adept at quieting the consciences of people who do not want to be troubled by feelings of guilt. In this instance they portray a God who has no moral absolutes. Either way, they manipulate people who have erroneous views of the character of God. Also, financial gain has something to do with the way they frame their message.

Christians need to know the dynamics of deception, because history has a way of repeating itself. "Everything that was written in the past was written to teach us" (Rom. 15:4).

The Good Minister: Timothy's Response to the Emergency

The good minister of Christ will "point these things out to the brothers" (vs. 6). Timothy is to present the truth in the form of warnings and instructions. If he does this, his message will have solid content. But first, Timothy is to nourish himself in the truths of the faith—"the good teaching that you have followed" (vs. 6). He is to have nothing to do with "godless myths and old wives' tales" (vs. 7). Always focusing on truth to the exclusion of error, he is not to give too much time to the repetition of false teachings. Concentration on truth will make it possible for his hearers to detect error.

Timothy must keep himself spiritually fit. "Train yourself to be godly" (vs. 7). The word picture suggests a workout in the gym. Paul does not belittle physical exercise, but he extols godliness as having "value for all things, holding promise for both the present life and the life to come" (vs. 8). It is not either-or, but both-and, with the preeminence given to the spiritual. The good minister keeps himself in shape both physically and spiritually.

The salvation enterprise is demanding, labor-intensive, "(and for this we labor and strive), that we have put our hope in the living God, who is the Savior of all men, and especially of those who believe" (vs. 10). The good minister firmly fixes the attention of his hearers on the Saviour and urges them to take up the cross. The most strenuous effort is required, not to produce merit, but to gain the most advantageous position so as to receive the maximum benefit that divine grace so freely provides. It will take strenuous effort to "throw off everything that hinders and the sin that so easily entangles" (Heb. 12:1). Paul will have none of that cheap grace that turns away from the path of self-denial. In spite of their show of religion, the false teachers at Ephesus took a casual attitude toward sin and morality. The good minister is not afraid to tell his hearers of the necessity for discipline.

The young Timothy is to command respect: "Don't let anyone look down on you because you are young" (vs. 12). But he is to gain this respect by his lifestyle and godly demeanor, not by verbal harangue. "Set an example for the believers in speech, in life, in love, in faith, and in purity" (vs. 12). The thoroughly converted minister carries an authority that no conference committee or board of elders can grant. If the minister does not have the authority that comes from a godly life—whether young or old makes no difference—the people will come to look on him and his ministry as an irrelevance. On the other hand, youthful church leaders who model the gospel in terms of verse 12 will be a powerful influence for good—a spiritual force to be reckoned with. The list of young Christians who through the centuries have made an impact on their generation is impressive.

But do not think of Timothy as a mere stripling lad. Most scholars believe he was between thirty and thirty-five at the time Paul wrote this epistle. Thirty was looked on as the age of complete manhood by the early fathers because of Jesus' age when He was anointed Messiah and began His formal ministry.

Verse 13 urges Timothy to focus on those ministerial duties that are foremost. "Devote yourself to the public reading of Scripture, to preaching and to teaching." Ellen White's comment is insightful: "The highest work of princes in Israel,—of physicians, of teachers in our schools, as well as of ministers and those who are in positions of trust in the Lord's institutions,—is to fulfill the responsibility resting upon them to fasten the Scriptures in the minds of the people as a nail in a sure place" (Francis D. Nichol, ed., SDA Bible Commentary, 2:1039).

Once again the veteran reminds the young preacher of his call to ministry, the day when the call was confirmed by a prophetic revelation, "when the body of elders laid their hands on you" (vs. 14). He must always keep this event in mind. The situation demands due diligence, absorption in ministry, for the preacher's own salvation and that of his hearers is at stake.

Thomas D. Lea summarizes well: "What then should be our strategy when we live in a world inundated with false teaching? First, we must expose the errors we oppose. Second, we must develop personal holiness to ensure continuation in integrity. The combination of exposing error and practicing truth is a powerful antidote to heresy" (*Lea*, 34:133).

In every age the demands are the same. Purity of doctrine and purity of life go together like twins.

■ Applying the Word

1. The false teachers in Paul's day claimed to be loyal Christians. What false movements exist in the church today (or on its fringes) that create a similar danger for God's people? What is your best safeguard against being deceived and falling away from the faith (see 2 Thess. 2:10, 11; Eph. 4:11-15)?

2. Make a list of the things Paul told Timothy he should do in response to the teachings of the false teachers. Which of these can you do? Which are you doing? When you respond appropriately to false teachers, are you fulfilling your office appropriately? How is such a ministry a blessing to others? What can you do to increase your effectiveness?

4. Doctrinal correctness seems to be one of Paul's great concerns. Why was this so important to him? Why should it be important to you? What can you do to increase your doctrinal correctness? What advantage will your orthodoxy be to the church? Is your own orthodoxy your responsibility, or should you leave such matters up to the pastors and theologians? Is the orthodoxy of the church your responsibility? What are the most constructive steps you can take when you see false teachings coming into the church?

■ Researching the Word

1. Look up the words *gnosis* and *Gnosticism* in an encyclopedia (the *Encyclopedias Americana* and *Britannica*, available at any public library, both have good articles). Paul also responds to the growing heresy of Gnosticism in Colossians. Read this short book through, comparing it

with what you learned about Gnosticism from the encyclopedia(s) and 1 Timothy. Make a list of the teachings of Gnosticism that Paul seems clearly concerned about. What would be the implication for your Christian faith and your walk with God if you believed these teachings?

2. With the aid of a concordance, look up the words *preach* and *teach* in the New Testament (also look up variants, such as *preaching* and *teaching* if you have time). Why does the Bible say these activities are so important to the church? In light of your study, what are the strengths and weaknesses of the teaching and preaching ministry in your congregation? What suggestions can you gather from the Bible for strengthening these ministries in your church?

∎ Further Study of the Word

1. For a helpful discussion on the conscience in the writings of Paul, see G. F. Hawthorne and R. P. Martin, eds., *Dictionary of Paul and His Letters,* 153-156.
2. For further discussion on the dietary issue in 1 Timothy 4:3, see F. D. Nichol, *Answers to Objections,* 423-427.
3. For more on Gnosticism, see G. F. Bromiley, ed., *The International Standard Bible Encyclopedia,* 2:484-491.

CHAPTER FIVE

Counsels on Social and Ethical Issues

1 Timothy 5:1–6:2

The apostle is about ready to bring his letter to a close, but there are still some important considerations—practical matters, ethical and social concerns—that he must discuss with Timothy. The church is a web of humanity, of lives that are bound together. Interdependence is the word. What affects one affects all. The pastor should understand this. His life has a greater impact on other lives than just about any other member of the church. To be careless and thoughtless in his relationships with people can prove disastrous. The pastor can put the entire community at risk. Therefore, discretion is the better part of valor. The preacher must not play into the hands of the enemy.

In previous chapters, Paul has exposed and sharply rebuked the false teachers. It is his duty now to affirm the loyal ones. Timothy is to be careful not to be partial or to play favorites. The apostle is covering all the bases. He includes everyone—male, female, young, old, leaders, widows, slaves. As a community of faith—the household of God—the members are to care for each other. Leaders set the pattern here also.

One other consideration comes up in chapter 5. Paul cautions Timothy to take care of his own health. He is not exempt from the laws that govern the body. He must not deplete his physical capital. All of the above Timothy is to model and teach.

Paul's counsel to Pastor Timothy is appropriate to today's church and its pastors. Recent studies indicate that people still have high expectations for the minister. The qualities that the apostle sees as necessary to pastoral ministry still apply today. Paul's list reads, "above reproach," "sensible," "dignified," "temperate," "hospitable," "gentle," "not quar-

relsome," "not a lover of money," and "well thought of by others." Today's list, based on the research, might read, "positive approach," "responsible," "flexible," "personal integrity," and "acceptance of clergy role."

■ Getting Into the Word

Read 1 Timothy 5:1–6:2 through two or three times, and then reflect on the following questions:

1. In 5:1-16 Paul offers counsel for Timothy's relationship to several groups of people. Identify each group, and enumerate the principles Paul sets forth for relating to each. What is Paul's "golden rule" for relationships within the congregation? Describe how these principles can be worked out in church and family life today.
2. What is "the list" in verses 9, 11? Were those on the "list" merely given a free charity ride, or did they have responsibilities to carry out? To the best of your ability, enumerate the privileges and responsibilities inherent in being on the roll.
3. What is the relationship of healthful living to spiritual formation? What relevance does Paul's counsel to Timothy about his infirmities have for us today? What are the implications for pastors and also church members as they attempt to reach their friends with the "right arm of the message"? Prepare a biblical statement on health and Christian witness.
4. Paul's ministry was self-supporting. Does this mean that all ministry should be self-supporting? Use the marginal references in 1 Timothy 5:18 to study this issue. See also Philippians 4:10-20.

■ Exploring the Word

Ethics for Christian Leaders

Paul begins this part of his letter by saying, "Do not rebuke an older man harshly, but exhort him as if he were your father. Treat younger men as brothers, older women as mothers, and younger women as sisters, with absolute purity" (vss. 1, 2). Paul's counsel on social issues shows that he has a good understanding of the dynamics of social groups. Interpersonal relationships can be a minefield. How do these people, with all their diversities, live in a community peacefully and harmoniously? The pastor is dealing with the fragile fabric of community. Some otherwise talented leaders never seem to understand what is going on as the group develops. The dynamics are constantly changing. New challenges and realities call for new approaches.

There is no "how-to" manual that covers all situations. However, some basics do exist. Treat every person as an individual of self-worth and dignity, deserving respect and having some spiritual gift to enrich the fellowship. The pastor should also recognize that each person has special needs. Leaders need to constantly improve their people skills.

The apostle lays down some ethical principles that Timothy must apply. The first of these has to do with the preacher's relationship with seniors in the congregation—how to deal with the elderly, to bridge the generation gap. "Do not rebuke an older man harshly" (vs. 1). Young leaders may have excellent academic credentials and an abundance of talent, but it is absolutely necessary that they be sensitive to the real needs of people.

The preacher needs "good antennae," an awareness almost approaching ESP. He must know how to develop rapport with all kinds of people. There is always the danger that young leaders in the press of duties may show impatience with an older person. No matter what the provocation, the members expect their pastors to be patient and long-suffering. When a leader "blows his stack" or comes across as arrogant in the face of tested experience, it diminishes his or her capital—the reservoir of congregational goodwill. This is unnecessary and counterproductive.

Another ethical principle has to do with Timothy's relationship to those in his peer group. The leader must realize that ordination does not elevate the minister above the flock. "You are all brothers" (Matt. 23:8). He must think carefully about these relationships with both male and female members, young and old. He is to treat "older women as mothers, and younger women as sisters, with absolute purity" (vs. 2). There are principles that gov-

ern the preacher's relationship with the opposite sex. If these are
ignored, the entire fellowship suffers. "Even an unintentional
breach of propriety can have serious demoralizing effects" (Oden,
120). But again, the leader sets the tone—the ambience.

Duty to Widows

Paul next turns his attention to the church's responsibility to
widows. "Give proper recognition," he says, "to those widows who
are really in need" (vs. 3). Widows cannot be ignored. The law of
providing for one's own covers widows. The Hebrew culture gave
widows status and provided what we today would call "social security." Israel was commanded to care for widows (Deut. 14:29;
24:17-21; 26:12,13). They were never to take advantage of a widow
(Ex. 22:22). Yahweh is described as a God who "defends the cause
of the fatherless and the widow" (Deut. 10:18). Israel's God is "a
father to the fatherless, a defender of widows" (Ps. 68:5). The
prophets thunder judgments against "those who make unjust
laws, . . . making the widows their prey" (Isa. 10:1, 2). Jesus was
severe in denouncing religious leaders who "devour widows'
houses. . . . Such men will be punished most severely" (Mark 12:40).
Finally, the apostle James, the living link to all that is vital and
authentic in Judaism, makes care for widows and orphans an expression of pure religion (James 1:27).

The apostolic church took their obligation to widows very seriously. Apparently there were many widows in the early church.
This gave rise to the first social crisis the apostles faced (Acts 6:1-7).
This potentially explosive situation was settled promptly by
proactive leadership. As the church grew and spread, the number
of widows increased rapidly. Some were aged and in dire circumstances, while others had well-to-do relatives who were expected
to care for them. Young widows who were vigorous and quite capable of supporting themselves were expected to do so. However,
another group of widows had come under the influence of the
false elders and had made themselves nuisances. "Not only do
they become idlers, but also gossips and busybodies, saying things
they ought not to" (vs. 13).

Thus the church needed guidelines and a "financial need test."
The widow must be "really in need" (vs. 3; see also vs. 5). She

must have been a faithful wife, "well known for her good deeds such as bringing up children, showing hospitality, washing the feet of the saints, helping those in trouble, and devoting herself to all kinds of good deeds" (vss. 9, 10). So, according to Paul, there are widows and there are widows. Leaders cannot afford to let the church assume the burden of caring for widows who do not meet the criteria for being placed on the "list."

That there was such a list is significant. Our English Bibles translate the word *katalegō* as "list." The Greek word means to enroll, to register, to select as a member of a group, to take into the number. It was used of soldiers, who enlisted and were inducted into the ranks. It was also used of persons who had been admitted to membership in a religious body. It is not far afield to presume that Christian congregations, in the interest of fairness and doing things decently and in order, developed a registry of accredited widows. These were in time regarded as having a special ministry.

Not only is there a financial need test; there is a character test as well (vss. 9, 10). Care must be exercised before placing a widow on "the list" (vss. 11-16). "Proper recognition" includes financial support. The mature, dedicated widow constituted an order of ministry in the highest sense. This is implicit in verses 9, 10.

Ellen White's comment illumines the discussion regarding women who perform this kind of ministry in our time (visiting the sick, looking after the young, ministering to the necessities of the poor). "They should be set aside for this work by prayer and the laying on of hands" (*Review and Herald*, 9 July 1895, 434).

Paul devotes considerable space to the problems of the widows and the possibilities for their ministry. He evidently feels that this situation with all of its potential for service (and also tension) in the church must be addressed wisely and forthrightly. Tremendous implications and insights for ministry exist here.

Respect for and Support of Leaders

While most of this letter is a condemnation of the false prophets, Paul does not want to give the impression that all elders are to be viewed with suspicion. So he adds, "The elders who direct the affairs of the church well are worthy of double honor, especially those whose work is preaching and teaching. For the Scripture says, 'Do not muzzle the ox while it is treading out the grain,' and 'The worker deserves his wages.' Do not entertain an accusation against an elder unless it is brought by two or three witnesses. Those who sin are to be rebuked publicly, so that the others may take warning" (vss. 17-20).

The church must protect the reputation of its ministers. It is their duty to provide financial support for full-time gospel workers. They perform a vital ministry for the congregation and are responsible for providing leadership for the church's mission. Paul takes an Old Testament principle and brings it over into the current situation. The hard-working ox is allowed to eat the grain he treads out. "In the same way," the apostle reasons, "the Lord has commanded that those who preach the gospel should receive their living from the gospel" (1 Cor. 9:14).

Although Paul had a self-supporting ministry, he never gave up his right to the financial support of the churches. He makes this clear in 1 Corinthians 9:1-14 with persuasive arguments: "Don't we have the right to food and drink? Don't we have the right to take a believing wife along with us, as do the other apostles and the Lord's brothers and Cephas [Peter]? . . . If we have sown spiritual seed among you, is it too much if we reap a material harvest from you? If others have this right of support from you, shouldn't we have it all the more?" (vss. 3-5, 11). The context is the situation at Corinth, where he is dealing with a particular circumstance, but the same principle applies in Ephesus.

However, Paul is not inflexible on this point, for at times he exercised this privilege. "I robbed other churches," he chides the Corinthians, "by receiving support from them so as to serve you" (2 Cor. 11:8). He was particularly pleased with the generosity of the Philippian church and regarded their gifts as "a fragrant offering, an acceptable sacrifice pleasing to God" (Phil. 4:18; see also vss. 10-17).

Who, then, should receive financial support from the church? Widows who qualify and are placed on the "list." Also, those persons who are assigned to full-time teaching/preaching ministries. The full-time servants of God's people need the recognition and endorsement of the fellowship as well as the call of God. In fact, all of the people of God are to be involved in, and are responsible for, the support of ministry, because ministry belongs to the whole church and not exclusively to the leaders. The true membership is all the people, under God, accepting their assigned functions for total service to the church.

The Stress Factor

Timothy's responsibility is the Ephesian Christian community. Among its members are Jews and Gentiles, all no doubt members of the various house churches in the city. Paul charges Timothy with the responsibility of administering the work of Christ in this great population center. This includes ministry to all segments of the community. His major assignment is to work with the elders of the churches.

In verse 21 Paul gives one of his summary challenges to the man he left in charge: "Keep these instructions without partiality," he says, and "do nothing out of favoritism." A minister who plays favorites is playing with fire. Feelings of resentment and anger can burst into flame at once or smolder for years. If the pastor is perceived as being captive to some group or family or individual, the church can be divided into warring factions. The wells can be poisoned. This rule must never be broken—no partiality, no favorites!

Therefore, Timothy must not "be hasty in the laying on of hands" (vs. 22). All kinds of people for all kinds of reasons will seek his endorsement of various projects and "ministries." He must weigh these matters carefully and not move too quickly. Influence is capital, also, and should not be spent foolishly. This includes the matter of recommending candidates for ordination.

When the apostle advises Timothy not to share in the sins of others (vs. 22), he speaks particularly about involvement with groups who might bring embarrassment on the cause of Christ. He is saying, in effect, Choose your associates with care, because you will be identified with them. This kind of thing can come back to haunt you. Therefore, "Keep yourself pure" (vs. 22). The apostle uses the Greek word *hagnos* for "pure" in this verse, the sense of which is, "Be open and aboveboard." The people are to know where he stands on the vital issues. Timothy cannot pander to any group. He is in no one's "hip pocket." His designation is "man of God" (6:11).

Paul spoke of Timothy's "frequent illnesses" (vs. 23). Ministry is, indeed, a stressful occupation, especially for one as conscientious as Timothy. He carries the people on his heart. He feels responsible for the spiritual welfare of the church. Tensions build, which sap the minister's vital energies and lower his resistance to disease. Stress is a killer. Paul knows Timothy's dedication and commitment. He also knows that the preacher's health is not the best. He advises him to take "a little wine because of your stomach and your frequent illnesses" (vs. 23). Wine mixed with water and taken for medicinal purposes would improve the young pastor's digestion. Pliny and others at that time recommended the medicinal use of wine in this manner.

We would not expect the apostle to recommend regular or even occasional social drinking (see Rom. 14:1; Eph. 5:18; 1 Tim. 3:2-8). In his last word to Timothy, he encouraged him to "keep your head in all situations" (2 Tim. 4:5). The word *nēphō*, which Paul used for "keep your head," means to be sober, to abstain from wine. Thus Paul is not advocating even the moderate use of wine. For medicinal purposes, yes. As a beverage, no. The biblical principle points toward abstinence.

Timothy probably tended toward overwork, failing to set aside regular periods for rest and relaxation. Too many long, uninterrupted stretches of intense ministerial activity could lead to emotional overload and burnout. As conscientious as pastors may be, they are not at liberty to sacrifice themselves for the cause. This would not make them "as living sacrifices, holy and pleasing to God" (Rom 12:1). They must guard their health as they would their reputation and their character. They need regular periods of rest and relaxation and an abundance of physical exercise as well if they are to be at their sharpest, freshest, and best at all times.

The Master Himself had pity on His careworn disciples and bade them, "Come with me by yourselves to a quiet place and get some rest" (Mark 6:31). This is the dedicated pastors' example. It is their reasonable service to care for the physical machinery.

The Use of Wine—a Perplexing Problem

The pastoral epistles confront us with a perplexing issue that does not readily yield to a simplistic proof-text approach for solution; namely, the use of wine. This problem must be viewed through the wide-angle lens of total Scripture. The whole counsel of God is the perspective. We must not make the text say what we want it to say. This is not correctly handling the word of truth (2 Tim. 2:15).

Perhaps a comparison with the Bible's teaching about polygamy will help us to understand better Paul's teaching on the use of wine. Many of the patriarchs had more than one wife, and the Mosaic law permitted divorce. Jesus' response to the Pharisee's leading question on this point was, "But it was not this way from the beginning" (Matt. 19:8). Thus the Christian is to begin with God's ideal world, the Garden of Eden. Here, God tells how He intended things to be.

The direction and thrust in Scripture is toward an unfolding, a reiteration, of God's original purpose and plan. All things point toward a restoration of the original order of things, the establishment on earth of a community that reflects the will of God and finally a return to the Edenic state. Jesus applied this principle to divorce and remarriage and, by extension, to polygamy.

Similarly, the total thrust of Scripture is against the use of harmful substances. However, God recognizes that we must live out our days in a world that is less than ideal. The Bible is not a cover-up. It is a case history of how God has dealt with very messy situations. Even good men and women were involved in actions of which God did not approve. "In the past God overlooked such ignorance, but now he commands all people everywhere to repent" (Acts 17:30). We must never mistake God's mercy as a sanction for transgression. His purpose is unchangeable. God has not lost sight of the ideal.

Alcoholism ranks near the top of social problems of our time. It has reached epidemic proportions. Being a member of Christ's church makes every believer an example to the world (1 Tim. 4:12). This is a tremendous responsibility. One cannot say, as one great athlete put it, "I didn't ask to be a role model." The Christian's lifestyle makes a statement that someone reads and takes seriously. William Booth decided that he must be a teetotaler because London was full of grog shops, and even little children were suffering delirium tremens. The responsible Christian position would seem to be total abstinence on the basic principle enunciated in 1 Corinthians 10:31. In a time of terrible need, the Christian witness ought, therefore, to come down squarely on the side of total abstinence.

Mature, growing Christians, who have put on Christ and taken on His attitude, do not need a plethora of proof texts to cover every possible eventuality that may present itself—and some hypothetical scenarios that haven't even taken place. The same Spirit who inbreathed Scripture is perfectly capable of making that word "living and active" (Heb. 4:12) in the experience of every believer as he or she determines to live out God's Edenic principles.

Reputation Precedes Arrival

Verses 24, 25 speak about reputation. The pastor must make all kinds of judgment calls about people. The pastor also is being judged. The Christian worker should know that he or she is under constant observation and evaluation. While reputation is not character, a good name is to be chosen above riches (Prov. 22:1). The people will discuss the leader before his arrival, and the people will make judgments. Timothy must take all of this into account as he interacts with people, especially as he is called to recommend church members for positions of responsibility. Simultaneously, he is to guard his own reputation jealously.

Good works precede the leader. His mistakes also go before him. Knowledge of the leader's strengths and weaknesses has a way of getting out. This is the immediate thrust of Paul's comments.

But there is a wider application. In light of the coming judgment of God (Seventh-day Adventists refer to it as the pre-advent judgment), it is prudent to send one's sins on beforehand by confession and repentance. In that day, unconfessed sin will bring condemnation. All sins will eventually show up at the judgment bar of God, whether confessed (those that go before) or unconfessed (those that trail behind).

Slaves and Masters—Another Perplexing Problem

Paul cannot overlook the question of slavery. The apostles preached the gospel to slaves, and many were baptized and accepted into the fellowship. Some historians believe that there were as many slaves as free persons in the Greco-Roman world. In the city of Rome, at one time, the ratio was one slave to every three free persons, and the ratio was probably greater in certain other cities. The plight of the slaves was pitiful.

Yet Paul does not lash out against the practice of slavery. He has already made his position clear elsewhere: "Were you a slave when you were called? Don't let it trouble you—*although if you can gain your freedom, do so.* . . . You were bought at a price; do not become slaves of men" (1 Cor. 7:21, 23). Paul was seized with the idea of freedom—total freedom of mind, body, soul. "It is for freedom that Christ has set us free. Stand firm, then, and do not let yourselves be burdened again by a yoke of slavery" (Gal. 5:1). "Now the Lord is the Spirit, and where the Spirit of the Lord is, there is freedom" (2 Cor. 3:17).

If Paul sincerely believes in the idea of freedom that he so fervently proclaims, why does he not urge Christian slaves to revolt? Why is he not more of an activist? He seems quite pleased that he was born free, even to the point of demanding his civil rights on occasion (Acts 22:25-28). Is he concerned only for his own freedom and not for the freedom of all human beings, especially his brethren and sisters in Christ? Certainly not. Every fiber in his being yearns for the total freedom of every person.

However, the apostle is determined not to precipitate a crisis by rash, impetuous actions. He knows the cruelty of Rome. Slave revolts of the first century were always followed by fearful reprisals with terrible loss of life and bloodshed. Paul cannot bear the thought of bringing bloodshed and suffering on innocent people. Only the explicit command of God can lead him to encourage this kind of action by Christians. The decision to openly rebel is not his to make. First-century Christians, while progressive in theology and social outlook, were pragmatists for the sake of the gospel. Paul's great fear is that Christians will come to be regarded as zealots.

The gospel of freedom that Paul preached eventually did sound the death knell of slavery. His personal attitude toward slavery is well illustrated in his treatment of the runaway slave Onesimus (Philemon). Paul encouraged Philemon to receive the runaway back into his household, not as a slave but as a dear brother (Philem. 15, 16). In 1 Timothy 1:9, 10 the apostle ranks slave traders with the worst of "lawbreakers and rebels, . . . those who kill their fathers or mothers, . . . murderers, . . . adulterers and perverts." His disgust and disapproval are unequivocal. There can be no doubt where he stands personally on the issue.

The Old Testament witness is also toward freedom and justice for slaves. The Israelites were not to make fellow Israelites into slaves (Lev. 25:42; 1 Kings 9:22). Fugitive slaves were to be given sanctuary (Deut. 23:15, 16). Kidnapping of slaves was punishable by death (Deut. 24:7). A slave who was maimed by his master was to be set free (Exod. 21:26, 27). The prophets warned the victorious leaders of the northern kingdom to return the people they had captured from the tribe of Judah and not to enslave them, "for the Lord's fierce anger rests on you" (2 Chron. 28:11).

There was also a provision in the law for the emancipation of slaves and indentured servants (Exod. 21:1-9). We have an actual historical account of this taking place in Jeremiah's day (Jer. 34:10). One thing should be particularly pointed out: The same commands that instructed Israel to treat widows with compassion and justice included also the alien, servants, and the poor. Yahweh insisted that Israel develop a social contract for the protection of slaves.

The entire testimony—the Law, the Prophets, the Psalms, and the added apostolic witness—is always squarely on the side of freedom and for the equality of all persons before God. The basis for this is creation and redemption (Acts 17:26; 10:28; Gal. 3:28). The Sabbath command summons the entire household, including servants, to join in common worship.

In the New Testament the believing slave and the believing master are members of the same household, the new Israel. The gospel requires them to treat each other as family members. The master also must keep in mind that he is not the landlord of ultimate concern. God's judgment of him will be based on his treatment of his less fortunate brothers and sisters.

Ellen White adds to the broader theological dimension when she introduces the demonic reality: "The whole system of slavery was originated by Satan, who delights in tyrannizing over human beings. . . . Satan is the originator of all oppression" (*The Southern Work*, 61). And on the eve of the Civil War, she said, "We have men placed over us for rulers, and laws to govern the people. Were it not for these laws, the condition of the world would be worse than it is now. Some of these laws are good, others are bad. The bad have been increasing, and we are yet to be brought into strait places. But God will sustain His people in being firm and living up to the principles of His word. When the laws of men conflict with the word and law of God, we are to obey the latter, whatever the consequences may be. The law of our land requiring us to deliver a slave to his master, we are not to obey; and we must abide the consequences of violating this law. The slave is not the property of any man. God is his rightful master, and man has no right to take God's workmanship into his hands, and claim him as his own" (*Testimonies for the Church*, 1:201, 202).

Time and place do make a difference. The same Spirit that impressed Paul to "soft-pedal" the slavery issue in his time inspired Ellen White to boldly advocate civil disobedience with reference to the unjust fugitive slave law of the United States of America.

■ Applying the Word

1. **How do Paul's counsels regarding widows apply to today's church? Why is the matter of caring for widows in the Bible coupled with care of the stranger and the poor? How does your church handle needy cases among its own membership and in the larger community? Does your church have a poor fund? How can we minister to the needs of people in a way that affirms their self-worth? Must help always be in the form of money? How can we be liberal toward the poor and still be wise stewards of the means God has entrusted to us?**

2. **What, if anything, should the church do about child ne-**

glect or child abuse in the congregation? Should the church do a background check on people who are being considered for church office? What should the church's response be if the person being considered for office is an errant father or a child-neglecting mother? How can the church best express its displeasure with offenders while still helping such people to develop into mature Christians?

3. How does your church affirm the pastor? Through monetary gifts? By scheduling an appreciation day? By doing whatever the pastor says without question? How should your church show appreciation for local church leaders and officers? How can you appropriately express appreciation to those who have labored long and hard in the service of the church, whether layperson, church officer, or pastor?

4. What is your church doing to make sure that all of the spiritual gifts in the congregation are recognized and fully affirmed? The term *glass ceiling* is current in business and industry. It means that some people, because of race, sex, or physical handicap, are limited to low-level jobs. Does your church have a glass ceiling for some of its of members? What should we be doing to make sure that every gift in the church is appreciated and developed to the maximum? Remember, a spiritual gift is a terrible thing to waste. How does the counsel to do nothing out of partiality apply here?

■ Researching the Word

1. The largest section in 1 Timothy 5:1–6:2 is devoted to a discussion about widows. Use a concordance to study God's concern for widows in both Old and New Testaments. What does this study tell us about God? What was the responsibility of the church to widows in Bible times? What principles in this counsel are eternal, and which ones applied in Bible times that do not apply today? What is the best way for Christians who live in coun-

tries with government-sponsored welfare and social security to apply the biblical principles of duty to widows?

2. Look up everything the New Testament says about slavery, including the entire book of Philemon. Also look up slavery in a Bible dictionary. What do you conclude is the New Testament's attitude toward slavery? Why does Paul's counsel on slavery suggest the "soft" approach of 1 Timothy 6:1, 2? How does his advice on the issue inform the modern church? To what extent does his advice apply to specific cases (or to the New Testament era) only, and in what ways can it apply at all times and under all circumstances?

■ Further Study of the Word

1. For insight into the Bible's teaching on the use of alcoholic beverages, see Roger S. Evans, "A Biblical Theology of Drinking," *Ministry*, July 1993, 12.
2. On the ministry of widows and support of widows, see Thomas C. Oden, *Interpretation—First and Second Timothy and Titus*, 119, 120, 150-159.
3. On the wine used at Cana and in Communion, see Ellen G. White, *Temperance*, 97, 98.
4. For Ellen White's insights into the issues and causes underlying the Civil War, see *Testimonies for the Church*, 1:253-260, 264-268.
5. On Ellen White's comparison of the emancipation of the American slaves to the liberation of the Hebrews and the demonic dimension of slavery, see *The Southern Work*, 41, 42, 61.

CHAPTER SIX

Parting Counsels

1 Timothy 6:3-21

Paul began his letter with a broadside against the false teachers at Ephesus. He concludes with a parting shot at the troublemakers. His focus is consistent. He has the errant leaders in his sights and refuses to be diverted from his main thrust. And now he turns the spotlight on the love of money that motivates these men. Apparently, with their smooth talk and show of scholarship, they had gained quite a following—and a good income.

The ancient world had its share of traveling prophets, called sophists or wise men. Some of these were clever orators who occasionally gained great celebrity. They worked at their craft and polished their act to perfection. Ephesus was a center of this kind of activity. Did the renegade Ephesian elders pattern themselves after these wealthy, imminently successful luminaries? This is certainly possible. Money and applause concoct an intoxicating brew—heady stuff. Paul's prayer is that Timothy's lifestyle and wholesome religious experience will stand out in well-defined contrast to that of these showy religious charlatans.

The conclusion to Paul's first letter is a marvelous example of effective review. The apostle picks up the strands of the various arguments he has used throughout the epistle and fuses them into a powerful closing statement. He uses a variety of arguments, scriptural references, literary allusions, and folk sayings, but these are simply variations on a theme.

Finally, Paul wants to focus Timothy's vision. He gives him a horizon that brings perspective. Photographers call it depth of field—something that is above and beyond earth's uneasy, passing landscapes. He brings into focus for Timothy the transcendent vision of the eternal world. If he can keep this real worldview, it will be for him compass and sextant. It will give perspective and light and a point of reference. It will take away uncertainty and give stability. It will give the young preacher a sense of direction and purpose and a vision that all the dazzling sights and alluring sounds of his bewitching age can never eclipse.

■ Getting Into the Word

Read 1 Timothy 6:3-21 at least two times.

1. The section of Scripture under study contrasts true and false riches. What constitutes true riches? Where did the false teachers "miss the boat"? How does Paul's counsel to the wealthy relate to the words of Jesus in such passages as Matthew 6 and 25? According to Timothy, how can wealth affect one's sense of values? How can we distinguish false from true riches? What is the one sure way for the wealthy to secure their goods? How does the wise man's counsel in Proverbs 23:23 relate to the question?

2. Review the characteristics of the false teachers that you have listed previously in your 1 Timothy notebook. Bring the list up to date in light of 1 Timothy 6:3-21. Note that their quarreling, controversial, and suspicious traits tend to reflect their heart condition, their real selves. What is the connection between those personality traits and the topic of money in the chapter?

3. List the attributes of God in 1 Timothy 6:15, 16. Note also Paul's response to those characteristics at the end of verse 16. How do verses 15, 16 and 1 Timothy 1:17 complement each other?

■ Exploring the Word

On True Gain

In the concluding section of his book, Paul goes back to the false teachers. "If anyone teaches false doctrines," he says. It is also clear in verses 3 to 5 that these same teachers have an unhealthy love of money. This has become one of their prime motivations. These people are spiritually sick for two reasons: their love of money and their fascination with (addiction to) controversies and quarrels about words. They have a morbid craving for controversy.

The apostle paints an appalling picture of the false teachers or any person who "teaches false doctrines and does not agree to the sound instruction of our Lord Jesus Christ and to godly teaching" (vs. 1). The Greek is very forceful here. Translated and paraphrased, it could read: "Such people have a problem. They refuse to consent, to draw near and submit to the sound instruction of Jesus Christ so that the truth can exert its saving power on their lives. Also, they are conceited, wrapped in a fog and swollen with blind pride. They have no comprehension of truth whatsoever, but rather they have a diseased appetite for disputes. They are always looking for a theme to debate, and they always jump onto trifles."

This futile activity, Paul says, is the breeding ground for strife, malice, contention, railing, vilification, spiritual degeneracy, and bad talk. It all winds up in evil surmisings and perverseness. Those who maintain their fascination with such arguments become spiritually rotten to the core in thought, feeling, and understanding. They have an acute case of *logomachia*—hairsplitting!

Paul goes so far as to say that the false teachers "have been robbed of the truth" (vs. 5). Notice the apostle's strong language: They have been robbed! They may at one time have been attracted to the gospel and fellowship with believers, but their reckless course of action has rendered them incapable of any sincere response to saving truth. God's judgment has already been pronounced on these deceived deceivers. Jude's description of them is appropriate: "They are clouds without rain, blown along by the wind; autumn trees, without fruit and uprooted—twice dead" (Jude 12).

The link between doctrine and conduct can be substantiated. Belief in falsehood leads to predictable outcomes. Sound doctrine, wholeheartedly received, leads to obedience of faith and godly living. Unhealthy teachings, on the other hand, cause friction in the Christian community, tearing the fabric of fellowship, the common bond that makes the people of God a family. That is why Paul is adamant—these people must be stopped, or the church will degenerate into a debating society whose members are clones of their fractious leaders.

The false teachers in Ephesus have finally reached the place where religion has become the means to an end, and that end is financial gain! But is it true gain? Paul thinks not, and he employs his best arguments to establish the point. "Godliness with contentment is great gain" (vs. 6). When seen in the light of eternity, material possessions are fleeting. Only godliness is imperishable.

Obviously, the false teachers have been doing quite well for themselves financially. The genuine apostles are those in want. But in reality it is the false apostles who have been duped by the enemy, robbed of the true riches. Godliness is a companion to contentment. It is priceless. "For we brought nothing into the world, and we can take nothing out of it" (vs. 7). Character is the only possession that survives. All else, like the mortal body, returns to dust. This is why the Christian is satisfied with the necessities of life—food and shelter. (Clothing is included in shelter.) The apostle has clear views of what life is all about. His values will stand up under life's stresses, because they have been tested in the crucible of experience and adjusted by the claims of Christ's gospel.

The Conceit and Self-Delusion of False Teachers

That the false teachers are making a deliberate attempt to enrich themselves through their heresies is evident from the words "people who *want* to get rich" in verse 9. The apostle is speaking about a mind-set, a disposition—the will to be rich at any cost. This is further evidence that the false teachers have sold out to the enemy. It is easy to predict that they will "fall into temptation and a trap and into many foolish and harmful desires that plunge men into ruin and destruction" (vs. 9). Paul is still talking about the false teachers. Jesus used the word *mammon* (money getting, avarice, acquisitiveness) to describe this terrible slavery.

It is the *love* of money, not money itself, that is the root of all evil. This intense desire for riches lures and ensnares its victims.

It is a setup for all kinds of get-rich-quick schemes that trap people in a cruel net with no way out! Covetousness is idolatry. The false teachers are impaled on this spear, and their predicament is exceedingly painful. Paul paints the picture as vividly as he can. It is a hideous portrait. This is the pathology of the false teachers—men once good who have gone bad!

Flee and pursue! Paul urges Timothy to "flee from all this" (vs. 11). But the young preacher is not to spend all his energies running from evil. He is also to flee *to* something. "Pursue righteousness, godliness, faith, love, endurance and gentleness," Paul says (vs. 11). There must be a goal to reach. Paul had a goal: "Not that I have already obtained all this, or have already been made perfect," he wrote to the Philippian believers, "but I press on to take hold of that for which Christ Jesus took hold of me" (Phil. 3:12). Christians are goal oriented. Ellen White says, "Godliness—godlikeness—is the goal to be reached" (*Education*, 18).

It could be expressed as life, liberty, and the pursuit of godliness. However, Paul's idea of godliness is practical, down-to-earth. It is not the easy bumper-sticker variety, nor is it otherworldly and ethereal. In the pastoral epistles it is deeds that count.

The Ephesian heretics want to cover their nakedness with a false asceticism—feigned spirituality, like the "whitewashed tombs" that Jesus censured (Matt. 23:27). There is a brand of religion that "protests too much." "Do not be overrighteous," the wise man cautions, "neither be overwise" (Eccl. 7:16). The false teachers were good at creating an aura of spirituality—a form of godliness. Their gospel was all propaganda and no fine deeds of righteousness.

The apostle urges believers to pray "that we may live peaceful and quiet lives in all godliness and holiness" (1 Tim. 2:2). In his view, "godliness has value for all things" (1 Tim. 4:8). It is "legal tender" for life's marketplaces and is acceptable in the world to come. Flee, pursue, fight, is the admonition. The goal, the prize, demands energy and perseverance. All the powers of mind, heart, and body are required. This was the only way Paul knew to live the Christian life—all out. Eternal life is the crown. It is a gift that must be taken hold of (vs. 12).

He reminds Timothy of the day of his baptism, when "you made your good confession in the presence of many witnesses" (vs. 12). Timothy's baptism was human recognition of his candidacy for immortality. His ordination, which provided human confirmation of his call to the ministry, was eclipsed by his baptism. The Christian's baptism is the door to the new world with its abundant life. His good confession moves the Lord Jesus to confess him before the Father.

Solemn Charge About Serious Business

Paul now gives the young preacher a solemn charge about serious business. He places Timothy before God, "who gives life to everything" (vs. 13). The Greek word *zōopoieō* means to revitalize, to make alive, to quicken. (*Quicken* is an old English word that means to "resurrect," "to make alive.") It is the life-giving God who creates and sustains and before whom we stand. Timothy understood what Paul was saying. In the presence of the One who preserves you, "keep this commandment without spot or blame until the appearing of our Lord Jesus Christ" (vs. 14). There is no discharge from the struggle against evil, which will continue until the appearing of Jesus.

The word that is translated as "appearing" (*epiphaneia*) points forward to the second advent, when Christ will be manifested in power and great glory. In common terminology, He will "show up." The timing of this event is in God's hands, which He "will bring about in his own time" (vs. 15). The emphasis is on the omnipotence and omniscience of God. History is His story. The timetable is in His hands.

Contemplation of the end of the story calls for another doxology, and this time Paul composes (or quotes) a hymn for Christians who must practice the presence of God in a pagan environment. We, too, are in the sight of this life-giving God. Nothing earthly, such as money or business or personal affairs, can be allowed to eclipse the vision. Again, this is the skyline, the point of reference—the consummation that God brings about in His own time. Satan would obscure this vision of reality if he could.

If this doxology was composed for the Ephesian believers, who were exposed to spectacular ceremonies in honor of pagan deities, it was most appropriate. For it was during Paul's time in Ephesus that the crowd in the amphitheater "all shouted in unison for about two hours: Great is Artemis of the Ephesians!" (Acts 19:34). Artemis, a female deity, was "worshiped throughout the province of Asia and the world," and had been given the title "divine majesty" (Acts 19:27). In addition, emperors and kings gave themselves preposterous and blasphemous titles. But as far as Paul is concerned, there is only one authentic Ruler, "the King of kings and Lord of lords, who alone is immortal and who dwells in unapproachable light, whom no one has seen or can see. To him be honor and might forever. Amen" (vss. 15, 16).

The humble believers in Ephesus could easily have been carried away by these impressive exhibitions of heathen deities. After all, the Christian community in Ephesus was made up of little house churches of probably 15 to 35 members each. Their gatherings for worship and celebration of the Lord's Supper must at times have seemed rather drab and unexciting, what with no skilled orators to give them an emotional "high" on Sabbath morning. But the apostle wanted to draw their minds away from the tinsel and glitter of this world to "an eternal glory. . . . So we fix our eyes not on what is seen, but on what is unseen. For what is seen is temporary, but what is unseen is eternal" (2 Cor. 4:17, 18). This is the horizon he wants to set for them.

They must understand that where two or three are gathered in Christ's name, by solemn promise He is in their midst. Let the gods of this world have their empty show. The Christian is in full view of the Creator of the universe. He is the supreme Benefactor, the Blessed One. All blessings flow from Him. He is the Ruler, the first Official of the *cosmos*. His authority is unlimited. He is sovereign King, the Foundation of power. His reign is without end. As Controller of universal affairs, He is worthy of all titles and is greatly to be respected. Dominion and lordship are His. He is absolutely immortal, dwelling in unapproachable light. No human being can fathom His greatness. All honor belongs to Him. Of highest esteem, He remains forever throughout endless ages, in perpetuity, the All in All.

The apostle distills these lofty thoughts and sublime expressions of wonder and awe into the lyrics of a powerful hymn. We can almost hear him saying, "When your neighbors extol their gods with great pomp and ceremony, sing this loud and clear. And as you sing, may our God be real to you, for you are in His sight."

Paul's postscript, his final word, is directed to the rich, the plutocrats, a term that suggests class consciousness, a snobbish attitude, an assumption that wealth is everything. Those who are wealthy in material things must not allow their possessions to make them blind to the ultimate realities. Priorities and values come into focus again: "Hope in God who richly provides us everything for our enjoyment" (vs. 17). The apostle does not condemn the wealthy. He urges them to place their hope in God. He has just set God before Timothy as the Life-giver. This is the only reasonable perspective.

So much depends on the right use of material things. Riches can be a blessing, or they can be allowed to obscure the vision. All human beings, Christians especially, are members of a charitable foundation—God's almoners. The way to secure eternal dividends is to place one's funds in the most dependable financial institution—the bank of heaven. How is deposit made? By doing good, by being "rich in good deeds" (vs. 17). Again, this is the continued emphasis in the pastoral letters—good deeds—not for merit but in the power of the Holy Spirit, who is the guarantor of our salvation (see also 2 Cor. 1:22; 5:5; Eph. 1:13, 14).

Wealthy Christians should regard sharing material goods as their special ministry. In the Bible, righteousness is made concrete through service to fellow humans. Christ accepts these deeds of kindness and love as if done to Himself (Matt. 25:40). This is an investment in which affluent believers can put their trust. All other investments are uncertain at best. Just as Christians are commanded to forgive as their heavenly Father has forgiven them, so they are expected to share the goods He has so freely bestowed on them. This is laying up treasure in heaven. The way to get a firm hold on "the life that is truly life" (vs. 19) is to break the spell of materialism. And nothing breaks that spell like the spirit of liberality—the spirit of heaven.

Paul is trying to help his wealthy brethren avoid the arrogance that characterizes the rich of this world—a foolish dependence on "wealth which is so uncertain" (vs. 17). He is also speaking to the church at large through Timothy. This testimony is to be read in the assembly. The less-than-affluent believers may also be under the spell of mammon and lose sight of real life and the fact that true life, eternal riches, is already theirs through Christ. Paul wants all believers, rich and poor, to "take hold of the life that is truly life" (vs. 19). But while eternal life is already ours, it can only be tasted, sampled, in the here and now. It remains for the consummation to bring Christians into full possession of what is already theirs. Immortality, the ultimate gift, waits to be conferred "in a flash, in the twinkling of an eye, at the last trumpet" (1 Cor.15:52).

Closing Words

The final word comes almost abruptly, without fanfare. "Timothy, guard what has been entrusted to your care" (vs. 20). The assignment has always been, "Deal with heretics. Don't let them steal away the precious truths of the gospel." There is a body of truth that forms orthodoxy, the word that can be trusted. Believed, received, and followed with the whole heart, "the truth" means health to the church—Christ's body—to each believer. These truths are worth guarding and even contending for.

It is just here (vs. 20) that the apostle uses the word *parathēkē*, which in its literal sense means something that is put down alongside, a "deposit," a fund, a sacred treasure held in trust. The term was used in the world of banking and finance. In this sense Timothy is a trust officer, and so are we.

The deposit, in Paul's view, is a tremendous treasure, a fortune, a gold mine. It is the knowledge of "the truth" that brings salvation (1 Tim. 2:4; 2 Tim. 2:25; Titus 1:2), revealed in Scripture (2 Tim. 3:15), and realized in knowing Jesus Christ (John 17:3). The deposit is related to the work and person of the Holy Spirit, God's gift "as a deposit, guaranteeing what is to come" (2 Cor. 5:5; see also 2 Cor. 1:22; Eph. 1:14).

"Godless chatter and the opposing ideas of what is falsely called knowledge" (vs. 20) will only confuse and disorient. The false teachers are exhibit "A." It was by dabbling into forbidden knowledge and so-called wisdom (sophistry) that these false brethren were drawn off course. They became fascinated and intoxicated with the unprofitable. Error is never harmless.

Paul's description of the situation at Ephesus is so well drawn that it continues to speak authoritatively to today's church. The community of faith is under orders. The Old Testament prophets' charge to people and leaders was always, "Be strong and very courageous. . . . Do not turn . . . to the right or to the left" (Josh. 1:7).

Paul's brief closing statement is reminiscent of David's charge to Solomon. After the old king had reviewed the specifications of the temple and cataloged his extensive accumulation of building materials, he turned to his son and said, "Now begin the work, and the LORD be with you" (1 Chron. 22:16).

Paul simply says to his son in the gospel, "Finish the job." "Grace be with you" (vs. 21).

■ Applying the Word

1. Research indicates that less than half of all church members contribute the largest portion of tithes and offerings. What are the spiritual implications of this for you personally? What are the implications for the church? What can you personally do to reverse this? What can you do as a member? What type of stewardship program would be most effective in bringing about change? What is the spiritual dimension of giving?

2. What is your responsibility as a member if a group infiltrates your congregation teaching what "does not agree to the sound instruction" (vs. 3)? How can you know when to speak out and when to be silent? Ask yourself, Am I sometimes silent because I do not want to offend? Am I afraid to get involved? If I am not responsible, then who is? How can the twenty-seven fundamental beliefs help me and my church in coming to grips with these issues?

3. What lifestyle issues do you see in verses 8 to 10? How can you avoid the extremes of opulence on the one hand and severe austerity on the other? As these words are

being written, an individual has just won $111 million in a super lotto. In an age that has gone mad over get-rich-quick schemes, what principles guide the sincere Christian? How can you know when enough material good is enough? If godliness with contentment is great gain, why is it so difficult for most of us to be happy with "great gain"?

4. What can the church do to make baptism more significant to the candidates and to the church? How can we make baptism the time of the candidate's "good confession" (vs. 12)? How can we make this ordinance contribute to the sense of family in the congregation? How can we communicate to the new member that he or she is a fully accepted member of the fellowship? How can baptism be made a seal of the believer's commitment to Christ? How can the day of baptism be made a kind of ordination for participation in the church's ministry?

5. Seventh-day Adventists, by virtue of their name, expect the second advent of Christ in the near future. What evidences do you see in the corporate life of the church and in your own family and personal life that this belief is still alive and well and influential? How does this major tenet of faith affect your lifestyle, attitudes, and behavior? Be specific.

6. Take the plunge! If you have not done so already, form a small group ministry unit for serious Bible study and fellowship. Ask the pastor's counsel. You may even be bold enough to invite people at the conference office to assist with resource ideas. (You may be surprised how eager they are to be involved in what is happening in your congregation.) You may even decide to use the issues addressed in the pastorals as the curriculum!

■ Researching the Word

1. Scan the Gospels, using a Bible that divides the text into sections with subheads. Look for major blocks, such as parables, where Jesus talks about money, wealth, ma-

terial goods, etc. What, according to Jesus, is the problem with money? What does He say are appropriate and inappropriate ways to use money? What are the spiritual implications of material wealth? List ways in which you have used money appropriately and inappropriately in the past. What changes does this study suggest you might make in your present use of money?

2. One of God's attributes is immortality. Use your concordance to discover what the New Testament has to say about immortality and eternal life. Make a list of the differences, if any, that you find between these terms. Is it possible to have one without the other? Does one come before the other? How does the Bible say we gain these experiences? What implication does this have for your everyday life?

■ Further Study of the Word

1. For an excellent commentary on characteristics of false teachers, see William Barclay, *The Letters to Timothy, Titus, and Philemon*, 123-128.
2. For insight on the folly of trusting riches, see Ellen G. White, *Christ's Object Lessons*, 255-259.
3. For information about God's immortality, see Siegfried H. Horn, et. al., *Seventh-day Adventist Bible Dictionary*, 521, 522.

PART TWO

2 Timothy

Passing
the Torch

Introduction to
2 Timothy

One of the best ways to study a book of the Bible is to read it thoughtfully from beginning to end as quickly as possible. In the case of the pastoral epistles, this will not involve a great deal of time. The following suggestions will help you to get the most out of a thoughtful reading of 2 Timothy:

1. **While not all Christians are called into full-time paid ministry, all are called to ministry. In 2 Timothy Paul is giving advice to a young minister. As you read his letter, look for ways that his advice regarding Timothy's ministry also applies to yours.**
2. **Like 1 Timothy, 2 Timothy is general counsel to a young minister. Paul touches on a variety of subjects. Make a list of these broad subjects as you read, and choose those that seem most applicable to your church and its leaders. Ask yourself what you can do to help your church apply Paul's advice to Timothy.**
3. **While 2 Timothy is not primarily about doctrine, Paul does touch on some important doctrinal points. Look for these as you read. Make a note of them, and reflect on those that are most meaningful to you. Especially ask yourself what Paul says that relates these Bible doctrines to Christ and your relationship with Him.**

The second letter to Timothy is Paul's last will and testament, his final legacy to his son in the gospel and to the church. It was written from prison as the apostle faced death by execution in what was apparently his second Roman imprisonment.

In 2 Timothy Paul draws on military terms and imagery. The Christian life is warfare. Timothy is an enlisted man under orders. His loyalty to his Commander must be unswerving. The dangers are still present and also the need for diligence and watchfulness. He is on guard duty, in the trenches. He must endure hardness as a good soldier. The man of God must keep himself a cleansed vessel "useful to the master" (2:21).

The entire letter is Paul's charge and a challenge to his successor to be strong, unashamed, because God has not given him "a spirit of timidity, but a spirit of power, of love and of self-discipline" (1:7). Chapter 4:1, 2 is unparalleled in its appeal to ministerial fidelity. This is especially evident in the fact that some of its words are so often used at ordination services. "I give you this charge: Preach the Word; be prepared in season and out of season; correct, rebuke and encourage—with great patience and careful instruction."

However, even in this intensely personal and highly emotional epistle, the theological side of the apostle shines through with gems of revelation, sublime and poetic:

> If we died with him,
>   we will also live with him;
> If we endure,
>   we will also reign with him.
> If we disown him,
>   he will also disown us;
> If we are faithless,
>   he will remain faithful,
>   for he cannot disown himself (2:11-13).

The need for constancy and faithfulness, even to the point of martyrdom, is the message of 2 Timothy. The inference is that it will take this kind of resolution and determination to preserve the gospel "deposit" intact (1:14). Paul can say this with great credibility because his life is already being poured out "like a drink offering" (4:6).

The message of 2 Timothy still speaks powerfully. John Calvin said that this epistle "has been more profitable to me than any other book of Scripture, and still is profitable to me every day; and if any person shall examine it carefully, there can be no doubt that he will experience the same effect" (see Oden, xiv). The times of 2 Timothy called for just the counsel, instruction, and encouragement that only the veteran apostle could give.

Outline of 2 Timothy

    I. Greeting and salutation (1:1, 2)
    II. Encouragement to be faithful (1:3–2:7)
    III. Hymn to Jesus Christ (2:8-13)
    IV. A workman approved by God (2:14-26)
    V. Godlessness in the last days (3:1-9)
    VI. Paul's charge to Timothy (3:10–4:8)
    VII. Personal remarks (4:9-18)
    VIII. Final greetings (4:19-22)

CHAPTER SEVEN

Passing on the Torch

2 Timothy 1

The truly great leader prepares successors. Paul has been in the eye of the storm for many years, and time is beginning to take its toll. He has borne the burden of leadership in carrying the gospel to the Gentiles without a break. Now, from a dismal prison cell, he senses that the end is near. His thoughts are of transference of leadership and transmission of the faith to the next generation. His focus in this, his last letter, is on the future leadership of the church. All along it has been his practice to train young workers, but the urgency is greater now.

Modern management strategies are just catching up with Paul's leadership concepts. "The signs of outstanding leadership appear primarily among the followers," says Max De Pree. "Are the followers reaching their potential? Are they learning? Serving? Do they achieve the required results? Do they change with grace? Manage conflict?" De Pree could be speaking at a conference worker's meeting, a faculty colloquium, a conference executive committee, or a local church council when he says, "Leaders should leave behind them assets and a lega-cy. . . . Leaders are also responsible for future leadership. They need to identify, develop, and nurture future leaders" (De Pree, 12-14). Ellen White put it insightfully: "We want every responsible man to drop responsibilities upon others" (Testimonies to Ministers, *302, 303*).

The church today has its task—to be immersed in mission. Central to that task is the transmission of the faith to the oncoming generation—something that goes beyond mere textbook knowledge. The toughest assignment is to pass on undimmed the flame and passion to share Christ and His salvation with the world.

The church at its best is intergenerational, self-renewing, and char-

acterized by a spirit of service. This radical service orientation that Paul modeled so well is his greatest legacy. The challenge remains unchanged for today's church.

■ Getting Into the Word

Read 2 Timothy 1 through twice.

1. What can we learn about Timothy and his family in 1:5-7? What are the implications of the word *timidity* in 1:7? What relationships might exist between *timidity* in this passage and Paul's repeated uses of the words *power, not ashamed,* etc., in chapter 1 and of *be strong* in 2:1? List any other evidence (direct and indirect) you can find about Timothy's timidity (*fear* in the KJV) in Paul's two letters to him.
2. What can we learn about the plan of salvation from verses 8 to 12? List the items, and describe the significance of each in a few sentences. Compare and contrast this passage with such great gospel/salvation passages as Romans 1:16, 17; 1 Corinthians 15:1-4; and Ephesians 2:1-10.
3. Look at the word *deposit* in verse 14. A similar expression is used in 1 Timothy 6:10. Compare with 2 Corinthians 1:22; 2:5. How do these passages complement each other? What are the similarities and dissimilarities? Is the "deposit" in Corinthians different from that in Timothy?
4. Check the reference to Onesiphorus in 1:16-18. How did this brother's concern for Paul affect the apostle? How did Paul express his appreciation for Onesiphorus's good deeds?

■ Exploring the Word

By the Will of God

In the introduction (vss. 1, 2), Paul again establishes his apostleship. He is "an apostle of Jesus Christ by the will of God" (vs. 1). He wants to assure his son in the gospel that the sovereign will of the Father undergirds the plan of salvation and assures its ultimate outcome in history. This is the God who makes promises and guarantees these promises through Jesus Christ. Thus the letter begins with God's plan, His purpose. With the outcome of the plan assured, Paul frames the apostolic greeting and benediction: "Grace, mercy and peace from God the Father and Jesus Christ our Lord" (vs. 2).

"I thank God whom I serve as my forefathers did" (vs. 3), Paul says. As he looks back on his long experience, he is thankful for his heritage—the faith of his fathers and the son in ministry that God has given him, to whom he can pass the torch of leadership. The God of Abraham, Isaac, and Jacob is also the Father of the Lord Jesus Christ. And the Christ of God is the Son of David according to the flesh.

Paul is proud of the role of pious Jews as keepers of the flame of the true religion. He has worked out this theme in the book of Romans. The apostle has been faithful in his assignment, and his conscience is clear. But Timothy is on his mind. He remembers the young preacher's tears (vs. 4) and wants very much to see him again. Timothy may have been with Paul when he said goodbye to the Ephesian elders at Miletus, when "they all wept sore, and fell on Paul's neck, and kissed him" (Acts 20:37). At any rate, Paul appreciates the young preacher's concern.

Now Timothy is the focus of his letter, the man to whom he passes the torch. He has always believed in Timothy's call. It is the manner in which Timothy carries out his assignment that gives him pause.

Timothy's Call and Preparation

Soon there would be a new situation for Timothy—Paul would no longer be available for counsel and companionship. Does the younger man have the necessary stamina and courage to carry out the assignment? Times of great distress are just ahead. Paul sets out to encourage and shore him up. Paul counsels his young associate to "fan into flame the gift of God, which is in you through the laying on of my hands" (vs. 6).

Timothy is assured that his call to ministry is in the will and purpose of God (vs. 6). Providence has ordered his upbringing. Timothy's father was apparently not a believer, but through Eunice and Lois, his wonderful mother and grandmother, who both feared God, he has a good heritage. Single-parent families and divided homes may seem to be at a disadvantage, but we must not despair. Timothy's experience is written for our encouragement. Lois and Eunice provided the demonstration of truth enculturated. Timothy chose to adopt it and make it his own against the odds.

Paul wants his son in the gospel to be conscious of the fact that it is God who has been preparing him all along. Paul urges Timothy to "fan into flame the gift of God" (vs. 6). Not that Timothy was on the verge of leaving his post of duty, but Paul knew that he was rather timid and retiring (1:7). He could wish that he were more aggressive, more forceful.

At some point Timothy had received his own call to ministry. He was equipped for ministry by "the gift." This gift of God must be stirred, fanned into flame by vigorous use. Gifts that are not in constant use will die. The gifts are for service. "Talents that are not needed are not bestowed" (White, *Welfare Ministry*, 101). With the gift comes the "spirit of power, of love, and of self-discipline" (vs. 7)—that is, the temperament, energy, and forcefulness to be effective. God equips His servants. He outfits them. The presence of the Holy Spirit adds a new dimension, something that cannot be explained in terms of talent, intellect, or human ability. So a man could say to the rough-cut, unpolished Dwight L. Moody, "I really can't see any connection between your talents and your success."

Love and Self-Discipline

"For God did not give us a spirit of timidity, but a spirit of power, of love and of self-discipline" (vs. 7). Two Greek words, *dunamis* and *exousia*, are translated into English as "power." *Dunamis* suggests force, ability, might, strength, abundance. This is where the word *dynamite* comes from. This is the word Paul uses when he says in verse 7 that God gives us "a spirit of power." Perhaps we can better understand what this implies by looking at some other uses of *dunamis* in the New Testament.

Jesus promised the disciples that they would "receive power [*dunamis*] when the Holy Spirit comes on you" (Acts 1:8). This became the norm for apostolic ministry—the Holy Spirit equipping the believers for witness. "With great power [*dunamis*] the apostles continued to testify to the resurrection of the Lord Jesus, and much grace was upon them all" (Acts 4:33). This power, resident in the Word, is released in the preaching of that Word as gospel. This is the meaning of Romans 1:16, where Paul calls the gospel "the power [*dunamis*] of God for the salvation of everyone who believes."

Without a doubt, the single most important lesson we can learn from these New Testament uses of *dunamis* is that spiritual power comes from God through the Holy Spirit. This power is not magical. It does not come through some mysterious occult experience, nor is it the release of some "spark of divinity" resident in us all that is activated when the right words are chanted. This power is not ecstasy. It is Christ's legacy to all His followers.

Exousia, the other Greek word that is often translated as "power," actually means authority, privilege, right, prerogative. It connotes jurisdiction and delegated influence. Jesus granted the disciples "authority [*exousia*] to trample on snakes and scorpions and to overcome all the power of the enemy; nothing will harm you" (Luke 10:19). Note that God's authority (*exousia*) in His followers is greater than the power (*dunamis*) of Satan. *Exousia* is always given for the upbuilding of the church. Paul speaks about the authority (*exousia*) that the Lord gave him "for building you up, rather than pulling you down" (2 Cor. 10:8).

In telling Timothy that God would give him "a spirit of power [*dunamis*]," Paul wants his associate to be aware of the tremendous spiritual resources available to him. He covets for the young preacher the boldness that should characterize the gospel preacher. This boldness is the opposite of timidity or cowardice. The early church prayed, "Enable your servants to speak your word with great boldness" (Acts 4:29). Their prayer was answered, "and they were all filled with the Holy Spirit and spoke the word of God boldly" (Acts 4:33). We have a key here to understanding Paul's theology of mission and service, his drive and enthusiasm. He wants to transmit all this to his son.

However, power without love is dangerous, and love without power is ineffective. Both power and love must be coupled with self-discipline to bear fruit that carries the approval of heaven (1:7). That is why Paul says that God gives "a spirit of power, [*and*] of *love.*" Then he added, "of self-discipline" (KJV: "sound mind"). Self-discipline is the ability to give a controlled response. It is the Holy Spirit again who gives the worker for Christ the ability to respond to any given situation calmly, with confidence and assurance. A line from Rudyard Kipling's popular poem of yesterday says it well: "If you can keep your head when all about you / Are losing theirs and blaming it on you . . ." But we are talking about something beyond human gifts and abilities.

Paul urges Timothy to seize the initiative, to be proactive and aggressive in his ministry. He is responsible for preparing and leading the church into active service. Every member is to be a front-line evangelist, effective in his sphere as Christ's witness. Timothy, then, becomes a key player, transmitting to the church the truth—the gospel—and also the commission to spread that word to others. At the same time he is to be a model of the qualities that make for true success.

Paul is writing this letter from prison. There is the possibility that some of the believers will be embarrassed because their leader is a prisoner. The enemies of the cross are no doubt making capital of this unfortunate circumstance. "So do not be ashamed to testify about our Lord, or ashamed of me his prisoner," Paul says (vs. 9). He is suffering for the gospel. This is honorable, for this, too, is in the will and purpose of God. Timothy is to be willing to join him in this suffering "by the power of God" (vs. 8). Paul uses an unusual word here—*sugkakopatheō*, which we see only in this verse. It means to suffer in company with, to be a partaker of afflictions. The apostle always looks on his suffering as joining him in fellowship with Christ. When we suffer for the sake of the gospel, we are in good company.

Saved and Called to a Holy Life

In one of his earliest letters, Paul wrote to the Thessalonian Christians that "it is God's will that you should be sanctified" (1 Thess. 4:3). Now, to Timothy, he says, "[God] has saved us and called us to a holy life" (vs. 9).

God's will and purpose are seen in the salvation He has provided, in justification and sanctification. Over and over, the apostle drives home to his young associate the thought that the basis of the plan is "his [God's] own purpose and grace" (vs. 9). It is the disposition of a gracious God to reach out to His lost creation. There has always been a reserve of grace to meet the emergency of sin, "from the creation of the world" (Rev. 13:8). But with the coming of the Saviour, a new dimension was added to the plan: "We have seen his glory" (John 1:14). What had been implicit has now become explicit, "revealed through the appearing of our Savior" (vs. 10). In the incarnation, the gospel enfolded becomes the gospel unfolded.

The plan calls for the destruction of death, which opens up the exciting possibilities of immortality, a life that measures with the life of God (vs. 10). This is the core of the New Testament message. "The reason the Son of God appeared was to destroy the devil's work" (1 John 3:8). "Since the children have flesh and blood, he too shared in their humanity so that by his death he might destroy him who holds the power of death—that is, the devil" (Heb. 2:14). "But Christ has indeed been raised from the dead, the firstfruits of those who have fallen asleep" (1 Cor. 15:20). The apostles literally rushed across continents to proclaim this good news: Death's stranglehold is broken! This gospel is new light and new life. Paul is proud to have been chosen by God to be a herald, apostle, and teacher of this message (vs. 11).

Paul is still attempting to strengthen Timothy's resolve. He adds his ringing personal testimony: "I know whom I have believed, and am convinced that he is able to guard that which I have entrusted to him for that day" (vs. 12). "That day" is the second coming of Christ. The believer places all that he has and is in deposit with Christ in total commitment, and He keeps it safe until "that day." We deposit with Him, and He deposits in us! We give Him our lives, and He in turn entrusts us with the saving gospel, "the pattern of sound teaching" (vs. 13). This is "the good deposit" (vs. 14). We are to keep it with the help of the indwelling Spirit.

Wholesale Desertion, Remarkable Exception

Paul could not understand how anyone could turn away from the source of real life, this great treasure, the fellowship that meant so much to him (vs. 15). It was like shortsighted Esau selling the birthright for a mess of pottage. Paul felt saddened by the defection of so many. Phygelus and Hermogenes stand out in his mind as the worst of deserters. But against this backdrop of desertion, one name is prominent above all the others, for which he has only praise: faithful Onesiphorus. This humble believer found the apostle in Rome—the big city—by perseverance and dogged determination. "May the Lord grant that he will find mercy from the Lord on that day!" (vs. 18). Paul seems to mention Phygelus and Hermogenes merely in passing, as if he is hastening to highlight the ministry of Onesiphorus as a shining example of loyalty.

The greatest of saints, including Paul, crave human companionship and sympathy. So did our Lord. Elijah needed to know that there were seven thousand in Israel who had not bowed to Baal. We need to resist the temptation to cynicism. In a sin-hardened world, God assures us that He has reserved a remnant for Himself.

■ Applying the Word

1. **What is the average age of your church membership? What does this say to you about the future? What is your church doing to prepare leadership for the next generation? On a scale of 1 to 10, where would you rank your church's success in passing the torch? Make a list of what you and your church are doing right. Make another list of what you could do better. List a few things your church might do that it is not now doing. Involve your Sabbath School class or small group in discussing these questions.**

2. **What is the church's responsibility to single-parent families? How is your church responding to this growing challenge? Which of the following describes your church?**

    a. "We don't have that problem."

    b. "We once had a few families like that, but they don't attend anymore."

    c. "I understand we have some families who need help, but I don't know who they are or what can be done."

    d. "I tried to help a family once, but it didn't do any good. They didn't appreciate it."

    e. "We already have a Dorcas society."

    f. "I really would like to get involved in that kind of ministry—how can we get started?"

3. What is your church doing to reclaim missing members? What have you learned in your study of the pastoral epistles thus far that might contribute to such a program?

4. Most of us feel more like Timothy than Paul. What is the best way to firm up our spiritual muscle? Can you think of any genuine Paul types in your church? How can the church make these persons available to encourage and assist the rest of the members to receive the spirit of boldness, power, love, and self-discipline?

5. How does true friendship, brotherly love, relate to the gospel and the golden rule? Requirement? Option? Where would you place brotherly love on the priority list?

■ Researching the Word

1. The best place in the Bible to do an intergenerational family study is in Genesis. Read the stories of Abraham, Isaac, Jacob, and Joseph in chapters 12 to 47. Pay careful attention to the positive and negative relationships between family members. Also note the character strengths and defects of each of these patriarchs and their wives. How did the relationships between family members affect the children in later years? What strengths did each family most clearly pass on to the next generation? What weaknesses? Joseph experienced unusual success in spite of the problems in his family. What

strengths did his childhood family have that can explain this? What strengths and weaknesses do you see in your childhood family? How have these affected your life in the present? What successes have you experienced in spite of the problems in your childhood?

2. Look up the word *power* in *Strong's Exhaustive Concordance of the Bible* or Young's *Analytical Concordance to the Bible*. Make a list of those texts in which *power* comes from *dunamis* (*dynamis* in the *NIV Exhaustive Concordance*) and those where it comes from *exousia*. Look up the words in each list in your Bible. What conclusions can you draw about the differences in meaning of these two words? What unique function(s) does each one have? How can you make each of these words real in your life? How does the experience of a Christian in whose life these qualities are functioning differ from the person in whose life they are absent?

3. Write down the names of as many Bible characters as you can think of in five minutes. Choose the two that seem to you to have been the most bold and the two who were most timid. Spend some time with your Bible, studying the lives of each of these characters. What were the strengths and weaknesses of the bold ones? What were the strengths and weaknesses of the timid ones? Is boldness always a good trait? Is timidity always a bad trait? What incidents in the lives of these characters best illustrate your answers to the last two questions? What are the spiritual consequences of these traits in both their positive and their negative aspects? How can you strengthen the positive aspects and minimize the negative aspects of boldness and timidity in your life?

■ Further Study of the Word

1. On suffering for the gospel, see William Barclay, *The Letters to Timothy, Titus, and Philemon*, 145-157.

2. On the Adventist attempt to transmit values to youth, see Roger Dudley and Bailey Gillespie, *Valuegenesis:*

Faith in the Balance, 57-79.

3. On guarding the deposit, see Thomas Oden, *First and Second Timothy and Titus*, 132, 133.

4. To learn more about religion in the family, see Ellen G. White, *The Adventist Home*, 317-325.

CHAPTER EIGHT

A Call to Commitment and Strength

2 Timothy 2

The major theme of chapter 2 is authentic ministry that makes a difference in the church, in believers' lives, and in the communities in which they live. The apostle continues to prod Timothy to "be strong" (vs. 1). His focus is on what it takes to hold high the cross, to be in the vanguard of the church's ministry. He uses some powerful, highly effective metaphors—the soldier, the athlete, the farmer, and the workman or craftsman. These metaphors illuminate various aspects and qualities of ministry that Timothy must seek to emulate.

The New Testament pattern is for certain persons in the congregation to be chosen to provide leadership and encouragement for the saints as they carry out the command to go and make disciples. Timothy is the prototype of this group of gospel workers. They are to be examples of ministry for the congregation and to the larger community. They are chosen to define ministry, what the church is to be about in the world. They are "to prepare God's people for works of service, so that the body of Christ may be built up" (Eph. 4:12).

Paul is keenly aware of the importance of this kind of modeling leadership. At one time the errant Ephesian elders probably showed promise and had been entrusted with responsibility. Could a closer scrutiny, some personality test or character profile, have detected a weakness or character flaw in these candidates that would have predicted their future apostasy? Is there a way today to detect "soul fatigue" so that the church can be spared future pain and trauma? We can only guess or hypothesize. Paul picks his metaphors carefully and urges Timothy to reflect on them. He assures his young colleague that "the Lord will give you insight into all this" (vs. 7).

■ Getting Into the Word

Read 2 Timothy 2 two times; then do the following exercises.

1. List the various metaphors for ministry that Paul uses in 2:3-7. Compare the metaphors in different Bible versions. Look up each metaphor in a Bible dictionary. What are the implications for each in the context of 2 Timothy 2?

2. Verses 15 to 19 contrast the approved and unapproved workman. What does the "word of truth" in verse 15 have to do with the argument in 15 to 19? Is the counsel in this chapter for ministers only or for all Christians? What evidence do you have for your answer?

3. How does the counsel in verses 20 to 26 relate to verses 15 to 19? Be specific. Make a list of the relationships, and expound upon each in a few sentences.

4. What are the two essential characteristics of the seal or inscription of verse 19? What is the relationship between the seal in Timothy and passages such as 2 Corinthians 1:21, 22; Ephesians 1:13, 14; 4:30; and Revelation 7:1-3?

5. Paul points out Hymenaeus as the worst kind of defector. Where else is this man mentioned? Is this the same person whom Paul "handed over to Satan" in 1 Timothy 1:20? If so, why is he still active in his opposition to the gospel? What does this say to you about the church's ability to effectively "banish" dissidents?

■ Exploring the Word

Preparation of Leaders

Paul opens the chapter with the words "You then my son *be strong*" (vs. 1). This charge reminds us of what Moses said to Joshua in turning over the leadership of the Israelite nation to him: "Be strong and courageous" (Deut. 31:7). Timothy would need all the strength he could muster. However, his strength and effectiveness were not in himself. Rather, they were "in the grace that is in

Christ Jesus" (vs. 1). This time Paul uses the word *endunamoō* (a derivative of *dunamis*), which means to empower, to enable, to increase in strength. There is enabling power in grace. The apostle confesses, "By the grace of God I am what I am. . . . I worked harder than all of them—yet not I, but the grace of God that was with me" (1 Cor. 15:10). Paul is saying something more to Timothy than "keep a stiff upper lip," or "grow up and be a man."

We as Christians need more than pop psychology and homiletical nostrums on the power of "possibility thinking." We need to be pointed to and connected with the enabling Source. As Christian soldiers, we need to find "the throne of grace," which we can approach "with confidence" and where we can "receive mercy and find grace to help us in our time of need" (Heb. 4:16). Our strength is "in the Lord and in his mighty power" (Eph. 6:10). This is the background of the senior preacher's counsel to his junior partner to be strong.

The counsel applies to Timothy first because he is the model minister, who in turn is to entrust to reliable men "the things you have heard me say" (vs. 2). These reliable individuals must be "qualified to teach others." A kind of apostolic succession is implied, not based on tradition but on faithfulness to the apostolic message. Authentic ministry has its origins in Christ's commission to the apostles. Under the terms of the new covenant, it is "not by name and lineage, but by likeness of character. So the apostolic succession rests not upon the transmission of ecclesiastical authority, but upon spiritual relationship. A life actuated by the apostles' spirit, the belief and teaching of the truth they taught, this is the true evidence of apostolic succession. This is what constitutes men the successors of the first teachers of the gospel" (White, *The Desire of Ages*, 467).

Paul continues to boost Timothy's morale: "Endure hardship with us as a good soldier of Christ Jesus" (vs. 3). This leads into the main section of his argument, where he gets at the heart of ministry with a variety of metaphors.

What do the soldier, the athlete, the farmer, and the master craftsworker have in common that is also common to ministry? Certainly commitment and a willingness to work hard and long. The military person must be loyal and courageous, willing to "endure hardship." Paul points out that "no one serving as a soldier gets involved in civilian affairs—he wants to please his commanding officer" (vs. 4). The athlete trains hard and "competes according to the rules" (vs. 5). The farmer expects to work hard to produce a good crop. He receives his share of the crop at the end of the growing season (vs. 6). Paul's challenge to Timothy is, "Reflect on what I am saying, for the Lord will give you insight into all this" (vs. 7).

Understanding the function and purpose of ministry from God's perspective is essential to the health and prosperity of the church. Ministry belongs to all the people of God. As democracy must have an enlightened citizenry to function at its best, so the church needs an intelligent membership that is willing to accept involvement and responsibility. May the Lord help the modern church to understand the dynamics that are at work in the body of Christ, which equip it and make it a powerful instrument in God's hands for the accomplishment of His purposes.

Now comes a sentence that seems almost parenthetical: "Remember Jesus Christ, raised from the dead, descended from David. This is my gospel, for which I am suffering even to the point of being chained like a criminal" (vs. 8). Paul reminds Timothy that his (Paul's) imprisonment is also a part of God's plan. God's work has not stopped just because one of its apostles is in chains, for "God's word is not chained" (vs. 9). Paul is willing to suffer even imprisonment for the furtherance of the gospel (Phil. 1:12).

Great Is Thy Faithfulness

The servants of Christ who serve well and "compete according to the rules" can expect a reward. One who is faithful has promised. Verses 11 to 13 could be the lyrics of a great hymn built on the strong promises of a faithful God:

If we died with him,
    we will also live with him;
if we endure,
    we will also reign with him.
If we disown him,

> he will also disown us;
> if we are faithless,
>   he will remain faithful,
>   for he cannot disown himself.

We hear echoes here of the Old Testament pen portrait of Yahweh, the covenant-keeping God. The Hebrew words for faithfulness indicate firmness, security, fidelity, stability, truth, trustworthiness. God's faithfulness undergirds and guarantees the plan of salvation.

Throughout Scripture, God is referred to as "the faithful God, keeping his covenant of love to a thousand generations of those who love him and keep his commands" (Deut. 7:9). Of Him alone can it be said, "There has not failed one word of all the good promises he gave" (1 Kings 8:56). His faithfulness is always associated with His love, mercy, righteousness, and forgiveness. The plan of salvation is assured because of God's faithfulness. He keeps His promises. His word cannot fail. The essential character of the Godhead is this: "He cannot disown himself." God's saving purpose is unalterable.

The Approved Worker

Paul now returns to the problem of the false teachers. "Keep reminding them of these things. Warn them before God against quarreling about words," for such quarreling is "of no value, and only ruins those who listen" (vs. 14).

It is in this context that Paul writes one of the most beloved passages for ministry in all the Bible: "Do your best to present yourself to God as one approved, a workman who does not need to be ashamed and who correctly handles the word of truth" (vs. 15). To entertain the godless chatter of the false teachers is to run the risk of spreading it through the body, like gangrene (vss. 16, 17).

Paul admonished Timothy to present himself to God as "a workman who does not need to be ashamed" (vs. 15). People like to watch a skilled artisan. Both their curiosity and their admiration are aroused. The worker is a study in concentration. He has an end in view. He knows what he is about. Timothy is to be like an artisan, professional in the best sense of the word, working with purpose and skill. He is to be a sharp instrument in God's hands.

Timothy is to be like a worker who "correctly handles the word of truth" (vs. 15). The Greek for this expression ("correctly handles the word of truth") is *orthotomeō*, which literally means to "cut a straight path." The approved workman follows the pattern. He uses sound words. He bases his message on the good deposit that has been delivered to him. He does not allow himself to be distracted. One cannot cut a straight line when turning aside to engage in debate over side issues.

Paul explains why it is so important that Timothy handle the word of truth correctly: Godless teaching (he calls it "godless chatter") leads to godless living. Paul identifies the teachers as Hymenaeus and Philetus (vs. 17), and he points out the particular doctrinal point that is in contention: "They say that the resurrection has already taken place, and they destroy the faith of some" (vs. 18). This is Paul's most specific reference to a false teaching. These men have handled the word of God deceitfully, mixing it with pagan ideas. This tendency to spiritualize the historical and factual nature of the Christian message has already been seen in 1 Timothy 4:1-5. The doctrinal system of the false teachers was based on the "new light" that Jesus' resurrection was the consummation and that the final events had already taken place—there was nothing to follow. Therefore, being in the new age meant that marriage was no longer appropriate, and, of course, God's people were supposed to abstain from eating certain foods (1 Timothy 4:3). The new earth state had already begun.

The resurrection is critical to Christian faith (1 Cor. 15:2, 3, 14). The apostles preached that it would take place at the end of the age (1 Cor. 15:51-53), which is the second coming of Christ. The Christian hope is the resurrection of the body. To reduce this great doctrine to the escape of an ethereal spirit from the body prison is a travesty of the gospel. It comes from Greek philosophy, and anyone who preaches it is not "rightly dividing the word of truth" (2 Tim. 2:15, KJV). Paul looks forward to the time when "the trumpet will sound, the dead will be raised imperishable, and we will be changed" (1 Cor. 15:52; see also Phil. 3:21).

Without the hope of a bodily resurrection, the doctrine of Christ is deprived of one of its most essential elements. No wonder Paul called this teaching gangrenous (vs. 17)! It eats at the vital truths of the faith. If we had only the words of Jesus on this point they would be sufficient: "Do not be amazed at this, for a time is coming when all who are in their graves will hear his voice and come out—those who have done good will rise to live, and those who have done evil will rise to be condemned" (John 5:28, 29). The resurrection is a vital part of the "deposit" that must be guarded.

God's Solid Foundation

Paul must be reflecting just now on the efforts of the enemy to overthrow the temple of truth. He rejoices in the assurance that "God's solid foundation stands firm, sealed with this inscription: 'The Lord knows those who are his,' and, 'Everyone who confesses the name of the Lord must turn away from wickedness' " (2 Tim. 2:19).

The pastoral epistles were written with the idea always in mind of the church as a household (see, for example, 1 Tim. 3:15). This house has a "solid foundation" (vs. 19). In 1 Corinthians 3:11 Paul points out that the foundation is Christ. In Ephesians 2:20 the church (house) is "built on the foundation of the apostles and prophets, with Christ Jesus himself as the chief cornerstone." In 2 Timothy 2:19 the apostle does not tell us precisely what the foundation is. From the context, we may conclude that he is attempting to convey the idea of the indestructible nature of the church and of all God's works. People need an anchor point, a structure that has "foundations, whose architect and builder is God" (Heb. 11:10), "a kingdom that cannot be shaken" (Heb. 12:28). What God has planted cannot be rooted up (Matt. 15:13). All the works of God are solid and well-founded.

Paul encourages Timothy that the work of God's church, "the building," will go forward in spite of Hymenaeus and Philetus and the defections from the faith that their heretical teachings have caused. Paul can be sure of this because a seal guaranteeing it has been placed on the foundation: " 'The Lord knows those who are his,' and, 'Everyone who confesses the name of the Lord must turn away from wickedness' " (vs. 19).

Every important civic building in Paul's day had its properly inscribed cornerstone. In this instance the inscription (seal) indicates ownership, "people belonging to God" (vs. 9), and purity. Those who belong to this household "must turn away from wickedness" (vs. 19). They are to be sanctified, set apart, cleansed as instruments "for noble purposes" (vs. 21). The house and everything that is in it belong to God.

Some scholars see in this twofold inscription a reference to the rebellion of Korah, Dathan, and Abiram, which was summarily settled by God Himself in as direct a manner as possible. When 250 Israelite leaders joined these men in their rebellion, Moses fell on his face and said, "In the morning the Lord will show who belongs to him and who is holy" (Num. 16:5). In settling the crisis, Yahweh showed two things: (1) He knows those who are His—He has the authentic roster of the saved, and (2) the Israel of God must separate themselves from the contaminating influences of rebellion and wickedness.

God's house is furnished with all kinds of articles, "not only of gold and silver, but also of wood and clay." Timothy and the brothers and sisters in Christ are to be articles made of "gold and silver," for Paul points out that the wood and clay are "for ignoble" purposes (vs. 20). "If a man cleanses himself of the latter" ("wood and clay"—vs. 21), he can be a noble instrument in God's cause. This metaphor is similar to the wheat and the tares or the good and bad fish in Christ's parables (Matt. 13:24-30; 47-52).

Paul's intent is that Timothy and all the believers in Ephesus prepare themselves for the highest service. The worker, the servant of God, aspires to do good work for his or her Master and therefore does not shun the necessary preparation and discipline. The approved worker will concentrate on the assigned task and avoid anything that would divert or distract from the mission.

Through the power of the gospel, Timothy is to purify himself of evil desires and "pursue righteousness, faith, love, and peace" (vs. 22). And he is not to engage in this work alone, but "along with all those who call on the Lord out of a pure heart." The entire church is to prepare itself for the highest service.

Paul explains just what he means: "Don't have anything to do with foolish and stupid arguments" (vs. 23). Workers who make a difference do not allow themselves to be involved in quarrels and disputes. In meeting opposition, the faithful servant never stoops to personal attacks on the proponents of error. "Those who oppose him he must gently instruct" (vs. 25). There is no place for rudeness or discourtesy in dealing with members and nonmembers.

The approved worker is a class act. He or she is the soul of gentleness. At the same time, there is a mental toughness born of discipline and commitment. Another characteristic of this approved worker is hope, a buoyant optimism. Even the false teachers, by God's grace, may repent and come back to the truth. It is not out of the realm of possibility that some may "come to their senses and escape from the trap of the devil, who has taken them captive to do his will" (vs. 26).

One thing further: Paul had pronounced a condemnation on Hymenaeus (1 Tim. 1:20). Apparently, Hymenaeus ignored the reproof and continued his nefarious work. However, Timothy is not to be disturbed, just as the church today must not be disturbed by the presence of dissidents in its ranks. The church has a duty to administer discipline, but it cannot wish these opponents of the truth to be wiped from the face of the earth. Some conditions will have to be endured until the end.

■ Applying the Word

1. **How can a leader avoid becoming irritable when individuals whom it is his or her duty to correct persistently refuse to respond positively to any and all appeals? How can the church deal with such people lovingly while objecting to their sin?**

2. **A group of people who have an "agenda" start coming to your church. They attend your Sabbath School class, and whatever the subject of the lesson quarterly happens to be, they find a way to work the discussion around to their point. Not only are their comments off the subject; they are contrary to the accepted Seventh-day**

Adventist fundamental beliefs. In a few weeks their distraction becomes disruptive. How should the teacher and the class handle them? Should the deacons be asked to usher them out? Should the pastor call the sheriff? Should the church doors be locked on Sabbath mornings and only trusted members be allowed in? What is the best way to protect the church, especially its newly baptized members, from the disruptive influence of false teachings and false teachers?

3. In verse 3 Paul counsels Timothy to "endure hardship with us like a good soldier of Christ Jesus." What hardships have you had to endure recently? What does it mean to endure them as "a good soldier of Christ Jesus"? In what ways have you done this, and what lessons have you learned that will help you to endure more like "a soldier of Christ Jesus" the next time you have to deal with a hardship?

4. In verse 5 Paul compares the Christian life to the competition of an athlete. Christians generally frown on competition because it so easily leads to hard feelings and false values. What specific spiritual lesson does Paul draw from his analogy of athletic competition? How can you apply this in your own life? Is competition always bad, or can it sometimes be good? Is it always avoidable, or do situations arise in which it cannot be avoided? If it is unavoidable at times, what is the Christian way to deal with it?

■ Researching the Word

1. In 2 Timothy 2:19 Paul refers to God's seal or inscription. With a concordance, look up the words *seal* and *sign* in both the Old and New Testaments, and review how the Bible uses them. What does the sealing mean in your personal experience? How can you know it is taking place? What outcome can you expect? Is the seal mentioned in Revelation 7:1-4 any different from what is described in other parts of the New Testament? How

would you defend your conclusion from the Bible?

2. Use a concordance to look up every occurrence of the words *mouth* and *tongue* in Proverbs. Write each text on a card, and group the cards according to the spiritual lessons they teach. What does Proverbs say that seems most relevant to the situation in Ephesus? If you could share your findings with the false teachers in that congregation, what would you tell them? What have you learned from this study that is especially useful to you personally? How might it benefit the church you attend?

■ Further Study of the Word

1. For more on the gangrenous nature of false teachings and the sure foundation, see William Barclay, *The Letters to Timothy, Titus, and Philemon*, 168-170; Thomas D. Lea and Hayne P. Griffin, Jr., in *1, 2 Timothy, Titus*, 216-218.
2. On Paul's suffering, see Thomas C. Oden, *First and Second Timothy and Titus*, 49, 50.
3. On the resurrection, see *Seventh-day Adventists Believe . . .* , 356-358.

CHAPTER NINE

Facing
Terrible Times

2 Timothy 3 and 4

In chapters 3 and 4 the prophetic lens is focused on last things, the end of the world, and the apostle's approaching martyrdom. He tells us what to expect in the end time, and he lets us in on his thoughts and feelings as he comes to the end of his journey. His tone is serious but not morose. Paul is not awash in self-pity. He seems to be in charge of his feelings. His interest in his brothers and sisters in Christ is still fresh. They are still in his heart, and he sends greetings. He looks forward to the end of the conflict and the ushering in of the kingdom of God in power and great glory.

At the same time, he is realistic. The time of his departure is at hand. The veteran has had his times of pressure, as all Christians must have. But he also sees an outbreak of troubles at the end time. "There will be terrible times in the last days," he says (vs. 1). Does he have in mind Daniel's time of distress, "such as has not happened from the beginning of nations until then" (Dan. 12:1)? Is this the time that Jesus referred to in His Olivet discourse, when He said that "men will faint from terror, apprehensive of what is coming on the world" (Luke 21:26)?

The Hebrew prophets envisioned a time of universal terror and woe just before the establishment of God's eternal kingdom. They called it "the day of the Lord" (see, for example, Isa. 13:6, 9, 10; Joel 2:1, 2, 11, 31; 3:14, 15; Zeph. 1:14; Mal. 4:5). The New Testament writers take up the theme (Acts 2:20; 1 Thess. 5:2; 2 Thess. 2:2; 2 Pet. 3:10). Jesus stands at the head of this tradition of prophecy, which theologians call apocalyptic. There are cosmic signs—the sun turns to darkness, the moon becomes like blood, the earth is convulsed with powerful earthquakes (Joel 2:30, 31; 3:15; Matt. 24:29; Mark 13:24; Luke 21:25; Acts 2:20;

Rev. 6:12). Christianity was born out of this view. As a Hebrew of Hebrews, Paul was steeped in these vivid apocalyptic pictures. The perils and dangers that Paul described and so earnestly warned Timothy and the early church about will be experienced again with greater intensity and on a wider scale at the end of the age. As he faces his own "last days," Paul looks forward to the day when he will receive the ultimate reward, the "crown of righteousness." Ellen White's tribute to the apostle in his last hours is unsurpassed.

> *Well-nigh a score of centuries have passed since Paul the aged poured out his blood as a witness for the word of God and the testimony of Jesus Christ. No faithful hand recorded for the generations to come the last scenes in the life of this holy man, but Inspiration has preserved for us his dying testimony. Like a trumpet peal his voice has rung out through all the ages since, nerving with his own courage thousands of witnesses for Christ and wakening in thousands of sorrow-stricken hearts the echo of his own triumphant joy: "I am now ready to be offered, and the time of my departure is at hand. I have fought a good fight, I have finished my course, I have kept the faith: henceforth there is laid up for me a crown of righteousness, which the Lord, the righteous Judge, shall give me at that day: and not to me only, but unto all them also that love His appearing. 2 Timothy 4:6-8"* (The Acts of the Apostles, 513).

■ Getting Into the Word

Read 2 Timothy 3 and 4 through at least two times, and then reflect on the following questions:

1. What does Paul mean by "last days" in 3:1? Is he speaking of his time, the final days of earth's history, or both? What reasons do you find in chapters 3 and 4 for your answer? List the characteristics of those days as given in chapters 3 and 4. What do you think is the most serious of those characteristics? Why? What other chapters and verses in the New Testament help you fill out your list

of the characteristics of the last days?

2. Paul's great charge to Timothy in 4:1, 2 has often been used in ordination services. What are the implications of that charge? How do these verses, in their context, relate to 2 Timothy 2:15 in its context? Explain.

3. Why do you think so much of the Bible is taken up with biographies? What teaching values do you find in biographies? Why does Paul keep asking Timothy to reflect on his life history—his "way of life"?

4. What Scriptures did Paul have in his day? What writings is he referring to when he says that "all Scripture is God-breathed"? What does Peter mean in 2 Peter 3:15 by "the other Scriptures"?

5. In some Adventist circles, we hear a great deal of talk about "the straight testimony." What was Paul's advice to Timothy on how to preach? What do you think he had in mind when he counseled Timothy to "correct, rebuke and encourage—with great patience and careful instruction"?

6. A number of Bible characters have left us their "famous last words," including Jacob (Gen. 49:1-28), Moses (Deut. 33:26-29), David (2 Sam. 23:1-5), Joshua (Josh. 24:14, 15), and Paul (2 Timothy 4:6-8). Why do we attach particular importance to the last words of significant people?

■ Exploring the Word

Godlessness in the Last Days

Paul uses the expression "last days" in chapter 3:1 to designate the final period of earth's history. This is the only instance in the pastoral epistles where the word *eschatos* is used. It means the farthest point, the final place, the end of, or the latter end. Keep in mind, however, that the New Testament church viewed the whole period of time between the ascension and the second coming as the last days. Sometimes the phrase simply means "in recent times" (Heb. 1:1) or "lately" (1 Tim. 4:1). However, the Bible writers seem to agree that there will be an intensification of every form of evil in the period just before the second coming.

This time is especially marked by the catalog of eighteen or nineteen sins introduced in verses 1 to 5. Sin ripens in preparation for the harvest (see Joel 3:13; Matt. 13:30, 39; Rev. 14:15-20). During these terrible times, "evil men and impostors will go from bad to worse" (vs. 13). Inordinate self-love is the taproot of the "vice list," the parent sin. The delineation is frightening—money grabbing, arrogant, abusive people who not only hate the good but eagerly embrace everything that is evil. "They will be unkind, merciless, slanderers, violent, and fierce" (2 Tim. 3:1-5, TEV). The concluding indictment in this list of sins calls for the severest condemnation: "Lovers of pleasure rather than lovers of God" (vs. 4).

What surprises us (though it shouldn't) is that the catalog includes "religious" people—the religious establishment, who have "a form of godliness" but deny its power (vs. 5). The Greek word *eusebeia*, translated as "godliness," is one of Paul's favorite terms. He uses it to describe holiness of character and deeds (1 Tim. 2:2; 4:8; 6:6, 11; Titus 1:1). It also refers to godly teaching (1 Tim. 6:3). The power of godliness is seen in the Holy Spirit's writing of the righteousness of the law on the hearts of believers. The spiritual malady that characterizes the last days is the *absence* of genuine godliness. Paul is evidently speaking about antinomianism, the teaching that the law of God was invalidated by the cross and superseded by the new "law" of love and grace.

Misinterpretation of Paul's teaching on grace has, through the centuries, led some Christians to set aside the binding claims of God's law. Antinomianism leads to license and leaves the Christian still a slave to sin. The function of law under the new covenant is the issue. "Shall we go on sinning that grace may increase? By no means! We died to sin; how can we live in it any longer?" (Rom. 6:1). Paul's dilemma was to establish the supremacy of grace without destroying the law. "Do we, then, nullify the law by this faith? Not at all! Rather we uphold the law" (Rom. 3:31).

The apostle is warning us here that we may look for the manifestation of the most blatant forms of antinomianism in the last days. In His Olivet sermon, Jesus said, "Because of the increase of wickedness, the love of most will grow cold" (Matt. 24:12). Throwing off the restraints of law was a problem in Paul's day, and it will be in our time. The sincere follower of Christ is warned against fraternizing with the no-law crowd. They are dangerously out of control. And what is more, their teachings are bewitching (see comment on Titus 2:11).

Still More on the False Teachers

The false teachers use religion as a cloak, a pretext, to "worm their way into homes," ostensibly to "counsel" women who are religious "junkies." However, their real purpose is to gain control over them.

In a male chauvinistic society, where females have been taught that they are inferior and that they must submit to men in all matters and suspend their own judgment, it is not surprising that some may have become dupes for male religious charlatans. The wonder is that so many women, even in ancient times, refused to accept the conventions and rose above "their place" that society would assign them. Nevertheless, the false teachers took advantage of the gullible, male or female, wherever they found them.

In this instance it was that class of women who "are always learning but never able to acknowledge the truth" (vs. 7). "They approach it [the Bible] as people approach a cafeteria, picking up the food that they like to eat, without much concern for a balanced diet" (Hall, 116). They will never know the liberating power of truth because they are not willing to be controlled by the Spirit (see Rom. 8:9). Submission to truth would have provided protection from the wolves.

The false teachers use the same method of operation as Jannes and Jambres (3:8), the magicians who resisted Moses' attempts to liberate Israel. It seems clear that the false teachers profit from human bondage. They oppose truth because it sets people free, and they want to keep people in a state of dependency. But their unscrupulous efforts to keep their followers in slavery will ultimately be exposed. "They will not get very far because . . . their folly will be clear to everyone" (vs. 9).

Paul's Ministry in Retrospect

The mentor now points to his own life as a subject for study. "You however, know all about my teaching, my way of life" (vs. 10). A good life is a powerful sermon. Timothy has witnessed Paul's "purpose, faith, patience, love, endurance, persecutions, sufferings" (vss. 10, 11)—the whole scene. He expects Timothy to learn valuable lessons from his observation (vss. 10-13), including the fact that even the greatest saint is not exempt from persecution and testing. This does not mean, however, that God's people are a hapless prey, for Paul adds that "the Lord rescued me from all of them" (vs. 11).

Evil men and impostors there will always be. In his Jannes-Jambres account, Paul suggests that seductive spiritualistic powers are at work. Paul has also seen the contrasting lifestyles of religious impostors. In other letters he has talked about principalities and powers and the "spiritual forces of evil" (Eph. 6:12; Col. 2:15; 1 Tim. 4:1). Ellen White also speaks of this trend: "The power of Satan now to tempt and deceive is tenfold greater than it was in the days of the apostles. His power has increased, and it will increase, until it is taken away. His wrath and hate grow stronger as his time to work draws near its close" (*Spiritual Gifts*, 2:277).

Paul explains to Timothy that things will go from bad to worse (2 Tim. 3:13), but the young preacher has before him the examples of his mother and grandmother, and of Paul, his mentor, before him. In their experience is ample assurance that the Word of God has saving power. "But as for you," Paul counsels, "continue in what you have learned and have become convinced of, because you know those from whom you learned it" (2 Tim. 3:14).

The Power and Purpose of Scripture

Paul reminds Timothy of his formative years: "From infancy you have known the Holy Scriptures" (vs. 15; see also Rom. 15:4). He has already commended Eunice and Lois for their successful transmission of faith to their son and grandson. We don't know what teaching methods they employed, but whatever they did, it was successful. Let the modern church learn a lesson, especially parents and educators (see Deut. 6:6-9).

God's great gift to Israel was the sacred writings, the Holy Scriptures. This distinguished them from their neighbors. Israel was a word-oriented community. Their God was Yahweh, the God with no image, who preferred to reveal Himself in words. Throughout Israel's history, God spoke through the prophets "at many times and in various ways" (Heb. 1:1). Then, when the proper time came, the unseen God spoke through His Son (Heb. 1:1). The God of the Bible reveals Himself through our sense of hearing rather than through our sense of sight! The Jews were called "people of the ear." Their God spoke to them. Everything depended on how they heard.

All Scripture can be traced back to God as its originator. His word spoken brings creation into existence (Ps. 33:6, 9) and also effects the re-creation of the soul: "For the word of God is alive and active" (Heb. 4:12, TEV). "For you have been born again, not of perishable seed, but of imperishable, through the living and enduring word of God" (1 Pet. 1:23). "Faith comes from hearing the message, and the message is heard through the word of Christ" (Rom. 10:17).

The quickening breath of God is in Scripture. *Theopneustos* is the word Paul used to indicate that the divine breath actuates the Word. God takes the initiative and sends communications to the children of men that maintain their freshness and vitality forever. "The grass withers and the flowers fall, but the word of our God stands forever" (Isa. 40:8). The dynamic in Scripture is released when the believer searches its pages for guidance and understanding, with a determination to obey its precepts. God-breathed, it is therefore "useful for teaching, rebuking, correcting and training in righteousness" (2 Tim. 3:16).

Teaching is the explication and amplification of its truths. To rebuke error is to reprove, to convict on the basis of evidence. To correct is to set the thing or the person straight, to reform or to rectify. The expression "training in righteousness" is from the Greek word *paideia*, which suggests tutoring, educating, or training. It also connotes disciplinary correction—chastening. There is also the idea of instruction and nurture. The Word is our tutor in the things of salvation. It is the agency that brings about the new birth. It furnishes us with instruction for right living and equips the believer in Christ to be a useful and effective servant.

However, the supreme function of Scripture is to bear witness to Jesus Christ. Jesus stated this clearly in one of His sharpest encounters with the religious establishment (John 5:31-39). The issue was, Who speaks for God? Who is the most credible witness? The scribes and Pharisees were skillful in debate, quoting Scripture voluminously to prove their point. Theoretically, they subscribed to the principle of *sola Scriptura*. But they missed the whole point of Scripture, its greatest organizing principle and the key to understanding it. Ten times in one paragraph (John 5:31-39) the word *testimony* (*marturia*) is used in various forms. In verse 31 Jesus was saying that while the people would not accept His testimony, "there is another who testifies in my favor, and I know that his testimony about me is valid" (John 5:32). John testified of Me, but "I have testimony weightier than that of John" (John 5:36). My works testify of Me—you have seen them. "The Father who sent me has himself testified concerning me" (John 5:37). "You diligently study the Scriptures because you think that by them you possess eternal life. These are the Scriptures [writings] that testify about me" (John 5:39).

So Paul could say to Timothy and to all who truly hear the Word, "You have known the holy Scriptures, which are able to make you wise for salvation through faith in Christ Jesus" (2 Tim. 3:15). "Now this is eternal life," Jesus said, "that they may know you, the only true God and Jesus Christ, whom you have sent" (John 17:3). This Word is given to ordinary people to be their most highly prized possession. Just as surely as Isaiah could say of the Christ Child, "To *us* a son is given" (Isa. 9:6), so may we say, To us the Word is given, incarnate and written. Ellen White insists, "The Bible has not been given for the benefit of ministers only. . . . *The Bible and the soul were made one for the other*" (*Signs of the Times*, 20 August 1894, 643, italics supplied).

It is clear that in 2 Timothy 3:17 the Holy Spirit is addressing us, the church of today, through Paul. He speaks to all of the members of God's household, "the pillar and foundation of the truth" (1 Tim. 3:15). It is the church, the whole people of God, who are to be equipped and outfitted to do the work of ministry. Timothy is a prototype, a representative of the people of God, chosen from among them. The ordained minister (Timothy) is to be judged on the basis of how well the members of his church are fulfilling their individual ministries.

How Shall We Preach?

Chapter 4 begins with a familiar form of Pauline address: "In the presence of God and of Christ Jesus" (vs. 1). This is an attention getter, the apostle's way of preparing Timothy for the serious message to follow. Remember that Paul is a herald (2 Tim. 1:11; 1 Tim. 2:7), and heralds blare trumpets that get people's attention so they can hear royal messages. The apostolic messenger is empowered to speak on behalf of the King as though the King Himself were present. He is authorized to speak about "righteousness, self-control and the judgment to come" (Acts 24:25). He speaks about Jesus, the One "who will judge the living and the dead" (vs. 1).

The next clause brings Paul's hearers into full view of the *parousia*—the Greek word for the second coming that emphasizes its power and the triple glory of Father, Son, and angels (Matt. 16:27)! Paul the herald trumpets, "I give you this charge" (vs. 2).

What is this message that calls for such an impressive fanfare? "Preach the Word" (vs. 2). Again, this is Christ's charge to His church. It is a great mistake to restrict this universal imperative to pastors, just as it would be a mistake to limit the terms of the great commission to the first disciples (Matt. 28:19, 20). This vital document that Paul calls Scripture is light and life for both the church and the world. Christ's church is the depository for this treasure. But the treasure is really for the world. The church is steward and not proprietor. Its mission is to communicate the Word. The mission is perennial: "Be prepared in season and out of season" (vs. 2). It is the function of preaching to "correct, rebuke and encourage—with great patience and careful instruction" (vs. 2). This is the application of the Word. Spurgeon used to say, "The sermon begins when the application begins." The preacher must relate all of this to life, for that's where the rubber meets the road! Otherwise, it will become an intellectual exercise.

Paul writes in an eschatological (end-time) context. "For the time will come when men will not put up with sound doctrine" (vs. 3). He has already called attention to a class of religious people in the last days who have a form of godliness but deny its life-changing power. Now he points out that these same people will tune out what they do not wish to hear. They will refuse to endure "sound doctrine" (vs. 3). Sound doctrine, or teaching, indicates more than simply *announcing* the Word. It includes *applying* the Word. This is what causes reaction—backlash. When the Word is applied, it demands response and decision, and this calls for radical change. This kind of change—reformation as well as revival—is painful. It calls for self-denial (Luke 9:23). People who love pleasure more than God are sure to react, sometimes violently.

Since chapter 3, Paul has been describing conditions that will prevail during the "last days" (3:1), with an emphasis on the religious community at that time who have "a form of godliness" (3:5). He deals with this same period in both of his letters to the Thessalonians. The focus of 2 Thessalonians 2:9-12 and 2 Timothy 3:1–4:5 is so similar that these passages should be read together. Christ's coming in power and glory will not take place until "the rebellion occurs" (2 Thess. 2:3). Then follows a period of intense demonic activity marked by the "all kinds of counterfeit miracles, signs and wonders, and in every sort of evil that deceives those who are perishing. They perish because they refused to love the truth and so be saved. For this reason God sends them a powerful delusion so that they will believe the lie and so that all will be condemned who have not believed the truth but have delighted in wickedness" (2 Thess. 2:9-12).

It is appropriate that Paul should conclude his final letter with a focus on the times just before the Lord's return. All of the major lines of prophecy meet and converge in the end time. They usually begin with counsel applicable to local, contemporary situations and then expand to encompass a universal situation. The prophecies of Daniel and the Revelation are prime examples. Paul wants both Timothy and his wider audience, the church in all ages, to be able to read the signs of the times. Thus they will have wisdom and strength to endure the stress. The obedient child of

God can discern the meaning of the times, even if he cannot explain it in words. This is how the fuller meaning of 2 Timothy 4:3, 4 is grasped.

Paul gets very specific in describing the days just before the coming of Christ. He says, "For the time will come . . ." (vs. 3). The Greek word for time here is *kairos*, which suggests a particular time that is pregnant with meaning. During this critical time, "men will not put up with sound doctrine" (vs. 3). Sound doctrine, as we have seen, is healthy teaching, the teaching prescribed by the apostles. It is also called godly doctrine. During this time, people will not endure godly teaching. This harks back to verse 1, where Paul's command is, "Preach the Word." People will have a longing, even a lust, for a watered-down gospel—entertainment in the name of religion. The word picture is of a people who hire religious teachers—heaps of them—to scratch their backs, literally to tickle them. They deliberately turn away from truth and close their ears so as not to hear it. Clearly, they prefer fiction, religious soap opera, to biblical truth. This is the ultimate rejection! And the judgment of 2 Thessalonians 2:12 applies: They come to believe the lies that they paid their "tuition" to hear. This is the "latter-day" meaning of verse 3.

The church is called to bear faithful witness to Jesus Christ, in season or out of season. This includes the final age. Faithful testimony to Jesus awakens opposition. All who would live godly lives (*eusebeia*) will suffer persecution (vs. 12). In the last fearful times, when evil grows to titanic proportions, the people of God will bear witness to Jesus at great cost. *Witness* comes from the Greek word *martureo*, from which we get the word *martyr*. Martyrdom is the supreme witness. In the final struggle, the saints will give their testimony in the face of fierce opposition (Rev. 12:11). Faithful witness includes declaring the whole counsel of God. "This calls for patient endurance on the part of the saints who obey God's commandments and remain faithful to Jesus" (Rev. 14:12). "Then the dragon was enraged at the woman and went off to make war against the rest of her offspring—those who obey God's commandments and hold to the testimony of Jesus" (Rev. 12:17).

Above all, it should be said that the church preaches also through her deeds. This is the consistent emphasis in the pastorals. By modeling the Christ life before the world, the church at Ephesus reaches the highest level of preaching, the greatest witness. Their godly life (*eusebeia*) furnishes irrefutable evidence that the Word has found residence in human hearts. This brings great glory to the heavenly Father (Matt. 5:16).

In verse 5 the apostle gives one last exhortation in light of the approaching crisis: "But you, keep your head in all situations, *endure hardship*, do the work of an evangelist, discharge all the duties of your ministry." The word translated as "keep your head" means to abstain from wine, to be discreet, sober, to watch. Those who are called to bear witness to Jesus must keep their heads clear at all times. Endurance is called for, bearing up in stressful times. Concentration on the work of the ministry will serve to keep the preacher focused and on course. Doing the work of an evangelist, pointing the people to the saving Lamb of God, in season and out of season, wonderfully clears the cobwebs from the mind. The appeal to Timothy and to us is to be faithful. "Discharge all the duties of your ministry" (vs. 5)—not just the pleasant ones, but the difficult and dangerous ones as well. And that includes the delicate matter of "rebuking" and "correcting" (3:16). The Commander-in-Chief requires loyalty to the end.

Valedictory

How a person faces death says something about the character, the "stuff," he or she is made of. But how does one face an untimely death—a violent end? It is one thing to die in bed, "being old and full of days," but to be taken from life violently, unfairly, in a manner reserved for the worst of criminals, must test the mettle as nothing else can. In this Paul achieves the ultimate identification with his Lord. "I am already being poured out like a drink offering" (4:6; see also Phil. 2:17). To pour out as an offering is to give one's self totally, without reservation. Christ's life was poured out as a holy drink offering on behalf of the entire human race. The drink offering was an integral part of the Hebrew sacrificial system. It signified wholehearted commitment and self-giving on the part of the worshiper in response to Yahweh's steadfast love.

"The time has come for my departure" (vs. 6). From his words we can see that the apostle is thinking clearly. He has his wits about him. He has not allowed death's approach to rob him of his reasoning powers or to dehumanize him. He accepts the inevitable. The master teacher, he passes on to his pupil a coherent, consistent, and realistic view of death. One does not come to this place in a moment. It is the fruitage of a well-spent life.

The great apostle approaches the end with dignity, a shining example in life and in death. What does all of this tell us? What do we pick up from the teacher? I would suggest the following:

- *Acceptance and resignation.* "As for me, the hour has come for me to be sacrificed; the time is here for me to leave this life" vs. 6, TEV).
- *Satisfaction.* "I have done my best in the race" (vs. 7, TEV).
- *A sense of achievement.* "I have run the full distance" (vs. 7, TEV).
- *Fulfillment.* "I have kept the faith" (vs. 7, TEV).

Paul's valedictory is also a carefully worded theological statement. He does not expect to receive the prize, the crown of righteousness, at death. The full reward awaits him, held in trust, until "that Day." The crown of righteousness is immortality, which will be conferred on the saints by the righteous Judge on "graduation day," at Christ's second coming. All Christians will receive their degrees at the same time—a profound truth that is in keeping with God's master plan, His great scheme of things.

In Paul's theology death was an enemy that would one day be overcome and annihilated. The cross and the resurrection assure this. Because they thought that death would deliver them from the loathsome "body prison," some of the Greek philosophers, such as Socrates, looked on death as a kind friend. But this is not the Christian view. Paul does not romanticize the issue. He never minimizes the reality of death or its devastating effects on the human family. But he knows the One who has conquered death, and he looks forward to the day when death itself will be destroyed (1 Cor. 15:24-28).

The apostle is not an extreme individualist. He is part of the body of Christ. All the members of this body are networked—or, as Ellen White often put it, "inextricably bound up together." Paul will have nothing to do with the view that sainthood is achieved only in a cloister, in splendid isolation. Not so! This glorious future with its great reward is "not only to me, but to all who have longed for his appearing" (vs. 8).

Personal Remarks and Final Greetings

In verse 9 Paul's humanness comes through, the personal touch that characterizes the genuine Christian. "Do your best to come to me quickly." He admits to loneliness. In the family of God, we need each other. We are not Stoics. Paul never lost his sense of family. His marital status may have been single, but his family and friends were legion. He is undoubtedly unsurpassed in cultivating friends.

When he loses a friend, it is a real loss. "Demas, because he loved this world, has deserted me" (vs. 10). He not only loves his friends, but he keeps track of their movements. He knows where they are (vs. 10). He quizzes everyone who visits him about how things are going. He thanks God for the blessings he has: "Only Luke is with me" (vs. 11). He can change his evaluation of a fellow worker: "Get Mark and bring him with you, because he is helpful to me in my ministry" (vs. 11). He kept up an extensive correspondence, and Tychicus is his letter carrier. He would like to have the greatcoat that he left at Troas, but he is more interested in his scrolls, "especially the parchments" (vs. 13).

The approaching end has not made him soft and sentimental. He still has a warning or two in him. "Alexander the metalworker" will bear watching, for he is a strong opponent of truth. The apostle admits also to feelings of rejection when everyone deserted him at his first trial, but he hastens to assure Timothy that he has no ill will for them. "We may be knocked down but we are never knocked out!" (2 Cor. 4:9, Phillips).

In his extremity he can still turn a phrase: "I was delivered from the lion's mouth" (vs. 17). The most important thing is that the message has been fully proclaimed, and the Gentiles have heard it. He has been promised safe conduct "to his [the Lord's] heavenly kingdom (vs. 18)" and rescue from attack. It is not unusual for Paul to break forth into fervent praise at midpoint in a train of thought. It is no interruption for him. Praise is always in order, so he says, "To him be glory for ever and ever. Amen" (vs. 18).

In verses 19, 20 the apostle sends final greetings to fellow workers and friends. This is never out of order for Paul, no matter what the subject. So he remembers at least four brothers and sisters and their families by name. He pleads with Timothy to come before winter sets in. And then, after passing on the greetings of the believers at Rome, he reluctantly pronounces his benediction: "The Lord be with your spirit. Grace be with you" (vs. 20).

■ Applying the Word

1. How should Seventh-day Adventist Christians relate to the growing tide of evil and immorality in the world? Should we try to influence society positively to change? Should we work hard for laws that will enforce biblical standards of morality? Since the only hope for permanent change is the coming of Jesus to destroy evil, should we give up on trying to convert a world that is irredeemable? Should we rejoice inasmuch as mounting evil is a sign that the coming of Jesus is near? Whichever answer(s) you choose, how can you become personally involved in making it happen?

2. What do Paul's words in 3:12 that "everyone who wants to live a godly life in Christ Jesus will be persecuted" mean to me? Have I experienced persecution for my faith? If not, why not? If I have, is the persecution in any way traceable to a flaw in my character? How can I know if the answer is Yes?

3. In what ways can those who are not involved in full-time ministerial labor follow Paul's charge to Timothy to "preach the Word"? How can I apply this charge in my own life? What does it mean to "preach" if I'm not an ordained minister or a licensed lay preacher? To whom can I preach and how? How can I preach without com-

ing across as preachy?

4. What is the relationship between the correcting and rebuking mentioned in 3:16 and that mentioned in 4:2? Is the church and its leadership responsible for rebuking people today? How can we do this without being offensive? How can we do it so that people will actually listen and take to heart what we say? What should be my response if I give a rebuke to someone and he or she does not respond positively? What should be my response if I feel an entire congregation is in error and they all reject what I say?

5. What was Paul's life like during the years leading up to his death that made it possible for him to accept his coming martyrdom so calmly? Am I living that kind of life today? If I were to follow Paul's example more closely, where might I begin?

6. Seventh-day Adventists by virtue of their name expect the second advent of Christ in the near future. What evidences do you see in the corporate life of the church and in your own family and personal life that this belief is still alive and well and influential? How does this major tenet of faith affect lifestyle? Attitudes? Behavior? Be specific.

■ Researching the Word

1. Use a concordance to look up all the occurrences of the word *persecute* in the New Testament, along with related words such as *persecuting* and *persecutor*. (You can also look up *martyr* and related words.) From this research, prepare a list of principles that can guide Christians who are under attack for their faith. Review what Revelation says about the persecution against God's people in the final days of earth's history. What principles does Revelation suggest that you didn't find elsewhere? How do the principles you found elsewhere apply to the kind of persecution Revelation describes? What do you suggest God's people can be doing now to

prepare for the time of trouble we believe lies in the not-too-distant future?

2. Scan through the Gospel of Matthew, looking for instances when Jesus reproved people, even if it was mildly, for errors in their lives. Also look for instruction He may have given about reproving sin. Try to identify principles that can provide guidance under a variety of circumstances to those who are responsible for giving reproof. Use the results of this research to respond to question 4 in the "Applying the Word" section above.

∎ Further Study of the Word

1. For insight into the inspiration of prophetic writers, see Ellen G. White, *Selected Messages*, 2:15-23.

2. For a good historical overview of how the Scriptures came to us, see Francis D. Nichol, ed., *SDA Bible Commentary*, "Languages, Manuscripts, and Canon of the Old Testament," 1:25-45; "Languages, Manuscripts, and Canon of the New Testament," 5:103-133; Ellen G. White, *The Great Controversy*, v-xii.

3. For the Seventh-day Adventist position on the inspiration of Scripture, see *Seventh-day Adventists Believe . . .*, 339-345.

PART THREE

Titus

Crisis in Crete

Introduction
to Titus

One of the best ways to study a book of the Bible is to read it thoughtfully from beginning to end as quickly as possible. In the case of the pastoral epistles, this will not involve a great deal of time. The following suggestions will help you to get the most out of a thoughtful reading of Titus:

1. **As in 1 and 2 Timothy, Paul wrote Titus to a young pastor by name, giving counsel on how to handle problems in his churches. However, Titus was a minister on the island of Crete, while Timothy was a pastor in Ephesus. Thus, Titus's problems would have been significantly different from Timothy's. As you read through Titus, look for both the similarities and the differences between his problems and the problems that Paul advised Timothy about. Try to think of ways that you can apply Paul's advice to Titus to your own life and to the life of your church.**
2. **Look for insights into the plan of salvation as you read through Titus, and especially how you can make that plan more meaningful in your own life. What does Paul say about justification and sanctification?**
3. **What does this letter say about God and His attitude toward people? What does it say about His relationship to sinful people?**

Titus is the third pastoral epistle in the New Testament sequence, even though chronologically it may have been written first or second. We are not sure. However, one thing is certain—

it belongs in the collection of pastoral epistles. It is addressed to a young pastor with counsel about pastoral and parish matters. Paul's purpose in writing the letter is quite clear: "The reason I left you in Crete," he says, "was that you might straighten out what was left unfinished and appoint elders in every town" (1:5). Organization is necessary. Order, system, and discipline must prevail if the church is to move ahead with a minimum of friction. Rules and regulations, though distasteful to some, are a safeguard.

Crete in Paul's day was a typical first-century pagan community—a rather large, densely populated island (some accounts say there were as many as one hundred cities and towns). Its people were known for their dishonesty, untrustworthiness, and even piracy. "The need of a thoroughgoing *sanctification* in congregational, individual, family, and public life had to be stressed here even more than elsewhere" (Hendriksen, 41, 42). Crete was not the kind of assignment most pastors would be anxious to receive!

However, Titus is the right person for Crete, for he has served his apprenticeship well. He was one of those entrusted with the responsibility of taking the famine-relief offering to Jerusalem (2 Cor. 8:16-19). From all we can determine, he was older than Timothy and came out of a Gentile background. While Paul advised Timothy to be circumcised (Acts 16:3), he resisted the suggestion of "some false brothers" that Titus be circumcised, interpreting such an act as an attempt to subvert Titus's freedom in the gospel (Gal. 2:1-5).

Titus seems to be more aggressive and forceful than Timothy. His assignment is to bind off the work on the island. Organization is incomplete; elders have not yet been appointed. But great care must be exercised in the selection of leadership. Paul's counsels to Titus are similar to the instructions in his first letter to Timothy.

There is some urgency for Titus to perfect the organization of the Cretan churches, because Paul wants him to come to Nicopolis as soon as a ministerial replacement can be found (3:12). The apostle also wants Titus to facilitate travel plans for Zenas, the lawyer, and Apollos, the eloquent and persuasive evangelist (vs. 13). But Titus's most important task is to instruct the Cretans on lifestyle, social matters, relationships with government, and relationships within the congregation and families. As the newly hatched chicken still has bits and pieces of shell that cling to its body, so the recent converts from pagan culture still have some carryover baggage from the old life that must be discarded. This will take some doing. Sanctification is not instantaneous.

Thus, Paul's counsel to Titus focuses on the felt needs of the community. The Cretan believers are to distance themselves from "those of the circumcision group" (1:10), whose tendency is toward rebellion. By God's grace they are to "say 'No' to ungodliness and worldly passions and to live self-controlled, upright and godly lives in this present age, while we wait for the blessed hope" (2:12, 13). There is an emphasis in Titus on good works (2:14; 3:14) and practical godliness. Paul urges both the Cretan believers, and us, to be a people "eager to do what is good" (2:14).

Outline of Titus

  I. Salutation (1:1-4)
     A. Identity and authority of writer (1:1)
     B. Basis of faith and knowledge (1:2, 3)
     C. To Titus (1:4)
 II. Titus's task on Crete (1:5-16)
     A. Appointment and qualifications of elders (1:5-9)
     B. Rebellious people must be silenced (1:10, 11)
     C. The Cretan problem (1:11-16)
III. What must be taught to various groups (2:1-15)
     A. Teach sound doctrine to the community (2:1)
     B. Motivation to godly living (2:2-10)
     C. Preparation for Christ's return (2:11-15)
 IV. Doing what is good (3:1-11)
     A. Subjection to authority (3:1, 2)
     B. God's kindness and love (3:3-8)
     C. How to deal with divisive persons (3:9-14)
     D. Closing remarks (3:15)

CHAPTER TEN

Unfinished Business in Crete

Titus 1

Paul's reason for living was to fulfill the apostolic commission—the establishment of the church in all parts of the world through the preaching of Christ. The apostles were given great authority to found the church of God. God wanted the church to be an indestructible fellowship based on the proclaimed Word and the Spirit-induced confession of those who came to faith. The ministry of the apostles was unique, authoritative, unrepeatable. They were the founders of the Christian church (Eph. 2:20). They received their authority from Christ and were His ambassadors with full authority.

Paul's claim to apostleship was constantly questioned and challenged, especially by the Judaizers—"the circumcision group" (Titus 1:10). These brethren followed him in his travels and made it necessary for him to continually reestablish his apostolic credentials. Regardless of how distasteful this may have been, he was not at liberty to diminish the full authority of his commission or the message he bore.

Paul's mission and message stand or fall on the authenticity of his apostleship. Titus's appointment and call to ministry are also tied closely to the legitimacy of the Pauline commission.

Paul's introduction to the letter is not that of a leader pulling rank or demanding his entitlements. The mandate is from God.

■ Getting Into the Word

Read chapter 1 several times. If you have access to a Jerusalem Bible, read from both it and the New International Version.

1. If you have access to them, use a Bible dictionary, atlas, and encyclopedia to find out all you can about Crete. Learn about its location, topography, history, people, and status in Paul's day. What can we discover about Crete from Titus 1? Check your concordance for references to Crete. What information do you find on Paul's contacts with the island? Who founded the Cretan church? If you cannot find specific evidence, make an "educated guess."
2. Who was Titus? Check the references to his name in the concordance. Is he mentioned in the book of Acts? Is it possible to draw a personality profile of this associate of the apostle? What was his experience before his assignment to Crete? In what ways were he and Timothy similar? In what ways were they dissimilar? Use a Bible dictionary to help you get your answer.
3. Compare the lists of qualifications for elder in Timothy and Titus. Look for both similarities and differences in the lists.
4. Are the troublemakers in Crete Jews or Gentiles? List the evidence you find in Titus for your conclusion. What is the meaning of each item on your list?

■ Exploring the Word

Well-grounded Hope

The introduction/greeting section to Titus is longer than the introductions to either 1 or 2 Timothy. Again Paul introduces himself as "a servant of God and an apostle of Jesus Christ" (vs. 1). He also presents himself first as a slave of God. ("Slave" is the literal meaning of the Greek word *doulos*.) Paul is God's slave but also Christ's apostle. As a slave he is committed to serve his King without reservations or questions. In fact, all of the apostles are called slaves of God (Acts 4:29). They acknowledge the total claims of God upon them in creation and redemption. He has exclusive rights. Yet they are also apostles—sent, commissioned, clothed with authority. Their assignment is clear—to build faith and knowledge in those who choose to serve Christ.

Paul's use of the word *elect* (vs. 1) should not confuse us. The Bible does not teach that some are elected to life eternal while others by some divine decree are doomed to everlasting destruction. The old deacon put it succinctly and correctly when he said, "God is voting for you, and the devil is voting against you. The election comes down to your vote." The elect are those who have cast their lot with Jesus Christ. They have already elected to serve Him. As for God, He is for us; He "wants all men to be saved and to come to a knowledge of the truth" (1 Tim. 2:4).

A "knowledge of the truth" leads to godliness (vs. 1; see also 1 Tim. 2:4; 2 Tim. 2:25). The apostolic message leads to right living. A correlation exists between doctrine and behavior. Certain teachings and injunctions in the "message" affect lifestyle and behavior. Ellen White put it this way: "The Lord, by close and pointed truths for these last days, is cleaving out a people from the world and purifying them unto Himself" (*Counsels on Health*, 106). In a sense this is spiritual surgery, circumcision of the heart, a molding and shaping of the character. There must be observable outcomes. When the apostle speaks about "a faith and knowledge resting on the hope of eternal life" (vs. 2), he means that this is the content and substance of the gospel message.

But there is another stage in the process—"the knowledge of the truth" (vs. 1). This knowledge is more than an accumulation of facts. In contrast to the "always learning" shallow experience of some of the Ephesian church members (2 Tim. 3:7), the issues of life are decided by hiding the Word at the center of one's being. The psalmist speaks about "truth in the inner parts" (Psalm 51:6). This is true discernment, spiritual eyesight. It is nothing less than the conversion experience, where truth overwhelms, conquers, and subdues the person. Indeed, it is the recognition that truth is personified in the person of Jesus Christ (John 14:6), who takes up residence in the heart. This is central to the entire apostolic message.

And always undergirding the message they preach is "the hope of eternal life" (vs. 1). The apostles and their successors until this day are authorized to offer a higher quality of life in the here and now. The life they offer is radically different from mere biological existence. This life begins when a person is joined to Christ (2 Cor. 5:17). The life hid with Christ in God has no end. "Whoever lives and believes in me will never die" (John 11:25).

Hope is one of the great New Testament themes, especially the hope of eternal life. This hope is central to Paul's thought. In Titus it is personified in Jesus Christ, who is the surety and guarantor of the plan of salvation (1:2; see also 1 Tim. 1:1).

Paul says that God promised eternal life to His people "before the beginning of time" (vs. 2). That is, it existed from eternity past. It was not an afterthought. God was not surprised by the emergency of sin. He did not *will* it, but He did *foresee* it. Then "at his appointed season" (vs. 3), in His providence and wisdom, He set up a timetable and revealed it by "bits and pieces" to His servants the prophets (Amos 3:7; Heb. 1:1), until finally, in Jesus Christ, it burst into blazing, life-giving light (2 Tim. 1:10).

In his Mars Hill sermon, Paul indicates that the Creator makes time a measurement for the working out of His plan (Acts 17:26). He also makes time finite, limited, in contrast to eternity, which is infinite, unlimited. There are limits and boundaries and probationary periods. God "determined the times set for them" (verse 27). He also makes time probationary. That is, it gives people opportunity to "seek him and perhaps reach out for him and find him, though he is not far from each one of us" (verse 27).

All of this is communicated in a proclamation, "The preaching entrusted to me by the command of God our Saviour" (1:3). This proclamation contains explicit directives for the believer—instructions that must be obeyed because they come to the church "by the command of God our Saviour" (vs. 3). It is apostolic and therefore authoritative.

Titus is the recipient of this authentic message and also of the authority to proclaim it. Paul wants the church on Crete to know that Titus has been given a ministry that is as heaven-endorsed as his own. Titus is a true son in "our common faith" (vs. 4). He is no imposter. Like father, like son. Having settled the matter of his apostleship and Titus's call, the writer is able to bring the greeting to a close with the familiar Pauline benediction, "Grace and peace from God the Father and Christ Jesus our Saviour" (vs. 4).

On Church Order and Governance

Church organization on Crete does not seem to be as advanced as at Ephesus. The Ephesian church appears to have been older. Furthermore, the Cretan congregations tended to be more Jewish, probably due to the dispersion of Jews from Palestine in great numbers during times of political unrest, famine, and persecution.

Crete was a good place for exiles to gain a foothold. Rome's presence was not so pervasive there as in the great cities of Asia Minor. These dispersed Jews always established synagogues, which became centers of religious, intellectual, and social life.

For one reason or another, the founders of the Cretan church were compelled to leave the island before perfecting an organization. The problem at Ephesus was false teachers who wanted to foist on the people a mixture of Greek philosophy and Jewish fables. The problem on Crete was also false teachers, especially those "of the circumcision." But the most pressing matter was the unfinished business of organizing to meet the crisis—the appointment of "elders in every town" (vs. 5).

The Cretan landscape was dotted with small cities, towns, and villages, and since the apostolic strategy was an urban one, it envisioned one or more house churches in every population center. The plan of organization calls for the appointment of elders to lead the congregations. The church was desperate for leadership, but, as in Ephesus, these leaders must not be rushed into office. There are qualifications for appointment to this ministry.

"An elder must be blameless" (vs. 6), a solid family man whose children are not open to the charge "of being wild and disobedient" (vs. 6). The opponents of the gospel, especially the Jewish critics, would be happy to embarrass the Pauline-endorsed leadership. The elder's entire family is on trial, including any slaves who might be in the household.

The elder has a solemn trust; namely, to protect and preserve the community against external attacks and internal erosions. This includes doctrines, beliefs, lifestyle practices, relationships, and whatever is contrary to the spirit of the gospel and the faith of

Jesus. The word for *steward* or *stewardship* is used here (vs. 7). A kind of management or administration is inferred, as in Jesus' parable of the faithful and wise servant who has been placed in charge of his Master's goods (Luke 12:42-48; Matt. 24:45-50). Faithfulness is demanded of such stewards (1 Cor. 4:2), and the degree of commitment increases with the size and importance of the trust (Luke 12:48).

Since he has been given a great trust—the care of souls—the elder must be "blameless, not overbearing, not quick-tempered, not given to drunkenness, not violent, not pursuing dishonest gain" (vs. 7). The terms of reference are explicit, and, to a great extent, have been stated in the negative, which is the most powerful form.

But there are also some positive statements: "He must be hospitable" (vs. 8). The refugee problem—Jews fleeing to Crete for relief from persecution in Palestine—has already been cited. Large numbers of these Jews, including converts to Christianity, found themselves at the mercy of their compatriots who were already settled in various parts of the empire. It was the duty of all Jews in exile to give shelter to their needy brothers and sisters. Christians—another persecuted minority in the empire—also adopted this practice. Elders would naturally be in the forefront of giving hospitality to strangers, especially Jewish Christians, who shared a Jewish elder's common heritage.

The positive list continues: "One who loves what is good, who is self-controlled, upright, holy and disciplined" (vs. 8). The decisive positive requirement is that "he must hold firmly to the trustworthy message, as it has been taught, so that he can encourage others by sound doctrine, and refute those who oppose it" (vs. 9). What is the message that he must have a firm grip on? It is the gospel he has received from Paul's pen and voice. This is the true, wholesome teaching in contrast to the unwholesome teaching of the false teachers. Their teaching is diseased and spreads like gangrene (1:11; 2 Tim. 2:17). The good doctrine that the apostle recommends produces healthy Christians whose lifestyle and demeanor are wholesome and upright.

Titus is to encourage those who are struggling to live by the true doctrine and conform their lives to its message. On the other hand, he is to refute those who oppose it. This message both affirms the obedient and exposes the deficiencies of its opponents, showing them up for what they really are. This gospel, faithfully preached, conquers sinners and comforts saints, as the old hymn says.

False Teachers Again

Titus's task is weighty. In the absence of fully authorized leadership, there has been mass apostasy on Crete, involving "many rebellious people" (vs. 10). It seems evident that in spite of their rebellion, the dissidents want to maintain their identity with the fellowship, if for no other reason than to gain influence over the gullible. As in Ephesus, these heretics are glib-tongued, eloquent, and persuasive. They are the Judaizers ("of the circumcision"—1:10), who miss no opportunity to straighten out Paul's "errors."

The Judaizers apparently know how to talk persuasively and make a great show of piety. They must have seemed quite impressive, but they are more talk than Christian action. They have to be judged by their fruit. And above all else, they have to be silenced.

The Christian community on Crete is clearly at risk, because "whole households" (vs. 11) are being ruined. The false teachers at Ephesus and the bad actors on Crete have at least one thing in common: They are out to get money (vs. 11).

Now Paul assumes the role of satirist. He uses the words of a Cretan poet to characterize the island's citizens: "Cretans are always liars, evil brutes, lazy gluttons" (vs. 12). This comes out in popular form as a ditty, "Liars ever, men of Crete, lazy brutes that live to eat." The apostle rather sarcastically quotes "one of their own prophets" (vs. 11) as authority for his indictment. (In the Bible the title "prophet" is normally reserved for those persons recognized and certified in Israel's history as having been called by God to speak to His people. In a sense prophets almost have to be "canonized." The apostles did not claim the title for themselves, and Paul certainly was not granting any pagan philosopher/poet authentic status as a prophet in the biblical sense. Had he been writing in English, he might have referred to one of the Cretan's "so-called" prophets.)

In any case, the apostle uses this stereotype of Cretan society as a whole to expose the dangerous methods and motives of the troublemakers. He condemns them out of their own mouth. This calls for radical surgery, without anesthesia: "Rebuke them sharply so that they will be sound in the faith" (vs. 13). The only hope of restoring such deluded persons is in the strong medicine of reproof and rebuke administered with apostolic authority.

At issue here is the use of the Old Testament, particularly the Mosaic or ceremonial portions. Most of the heresies plaguing the Cretan Christian community are Jewish. The Judaizers have been belligerent in their denial that any portion of Judaism and its many rules and regulations were set aside by the death of Jesus.

Elsewhere in the New Testament, Paul recognizes some value in the ceremonial parts of the law and admits that their role in Jewish history, while restricted, was glorious and beneficial (2 Cor. 3:6-11; Gal. 3:19-25). The problem is in what the circumcision party understands to be the basic purpose of the law. They want to make law a system of salvation, a means of producing righteousness, a method of obtaining merit. This was never the purpose of law in any of its forms, ceremonial or moral.

Israel had a long history of contending theologies. Rabbis established schools of disciples who were expected to defend and propound their theories. It is reasonable to assume that among the large number of refugees now in Crete, every stripe of Jewish thought and doctrine is represented. Add to that the contentious spirit that characterized the disputants, and Titus has a problem of monumental proportions. Again, this is why the selection of elders is so important, lest they become a part of the problem instead of the solution to the problem. Picture the members of the house churches invaded by refugees with whom they can identify emotionally, culturally, and ethnically. When these refugees begin to "show their hand," they must be silenced by the host in the house church—the elder. It is not difficult to imagine the trauma the Judaizers would have created in these small assemblies.

Some of these people have even substituted attention to Jewish scruples (kosher foods, ritual cleansings) for morality. But to Paul, Christianity demands not only that converts learn the new way but that they unlearn old beliefs and distance themselves from everything that is contrary to the gospel. Apparently this is too painful for some Christians in Crete, but Paul is uncompromising. It is impossible to be a true follower of Christ without shaking off this dead past.

The rituals and taboos have such a hold on some of the members that everything has become impure (1:15; see also Col. 2:20-23). But the Christian who has been liberated by Christ understands that moral purity is obtained only by and through the blood of Jesus. There is no salvation in ritual purifications and ceremonial washings. All the ceremonial ablutions of the sacrificial system cannot remove a single sin or purify the conscience (Heb. 9:9, 10). Christianity is a matter of the heart, and the conscience and purity or impurity do not depend on externals. Righteousness within will be seen in righteousness without, but legalism always attaches undue importance to ceremonies and rituals. One lives in mortal fear of being defiled even by casual contact with some forbidden matter. With the Judaizers, "nothing is pure" (vs. 15).

Without a clear concept of the character of God, the nature of sin, and the use of the provision that has been made for moral cleansing, the conscience becomes corrupt, nonfunctional, or malfunctional. Whether Jew or Gentile, the end result is a depraved mind (Rom. 1:28). With uncommon severity, Paul pronounces this class "detestable, disobedient, and unfit for doing anything good" (vs. 16). In what follows in this epistle, we shall see the need for such harshness and severity.

∎ Applying the Word

1. **How does your church care for visitors from Sabbath to Sabbath? Have you opened your home to strangers who have attended your church services? How can you help to improve the hospitality in your congregation? In what ways can the New Testament counsels on hospitality and the entertainment of strangers be worked out in today's world?**

2. **Which is worse, to choose an unqualified person to be**

elder or to appoint no elder at all? Is it appropriate to choose a solid Christian woman to be the elder of a church? Is it appropriate to appoint women elders along with men? What is your church doing to address this issue? What problems has your church encountered in the appointment of women elders? How are you working through this situation?

3. What is the relationship between stewardship and church administration (think of stewardship as a trust—vs. 7)? How can your understanding of the gospel be understood as a stewardship or trust (1 Tim. 1:11; Gal.2:7; 1 Cor. 4:1; 1 Thess. 2:4)? What is the relationship between stewardship and ministry (1 Peter 4:10, 11)? Where do spiritual gifts come into the picture of stewardship and service (ministry)? How are you working out your stewardship responsibilities, especially in sharing the gospel?

4. How is this matter of servant leadership working out in your church? How is it working out in your own life? How well are you and your church modeling Christ's challenge to the disciples in Matthew 20:25-28? What impact do you think a church like this would have on the world? How can your congregation become that kind of church? How important is this to you?

■ Researching the Word

1. Paul's list of qualifications for elders suggests that elders in New Testament times often held church services in their own homes. Find all the references to house churches in the Pauline epistles (look under the words *house* and *church* in a concordance). Check also the comments about house churches in the *SDA Bible Commentary* under Romans 16:5 and Philemon 2. Purchase a book about small-group ministry at your Adventist Book Center or other Christian bookstore nearest you (see suggestions in the "Further Study of the Word" section below), and from it identify the advantages that New

Testament Christians would have experienced by meeting in small home groups. How can Christians today, who usually meet in larger congregations, experience the advantages of house churches? What can you do to make this happen in the church you attend?

2. Purchase a book on conflict management in churches (see suggestions in the "Further Study of the Word" section below). Read it through carefully, and compare the advice it gives with Paul's advice for managing the conflict created by false teachers in Ephesus and Crete. What conflicts are alive at the present time in the church you attend? From the advice in the pastoral epistles and in the book you read, what suggestions can you offer for dealing with your own church's problems?

■ Further Study of the Word

1. For general information on Titus, see Francis D. Nichol, ed., *Seventh-day Adventist Bible Commentary*, 7:355-357, "Introduction to Titus."

2. For information about Crete, see Siegfried H. Horn, et. al., *Seventh-day Adventist Bible Dictionary*, 249, 250, s.v. "Crete"; *Harper's Bible Dictionary*, 193, 194, s.v. "Crete."

3. For information on small groups, see Michael Leno, *Bible Stories for Small Groups* (Pacific Press, 1991); Kurt Johnson, *Small Group Outreach* (Review and Herald, 1991); W. Clarence Schilt, *Dynamic Small Groups* (Review and Herald, 1992).

4. For information on conflict management in local churches, see L. Randolph Lowry and Richard W. Meyers, *Conflict Management and Counseling*, series editor Gary Collins (Dallas: Word Inc., 1981); Kenneth C. Haugk, *Antagonists in the Church* (Minneapolis, Minn.: Augsburg Press, 1988). The book by Lowry and Meyers explains the mediation process and is especially helpful for congregations in which there is a willingness to resolve conflict; the book by Haugk is helpful for dealing with people who have no desire to resolve conflict.

CHAPTER ELEVEN

Teach
These Things

Titus 2

As Paul wrote he had the family in mind—not the nuclear family of the late twentieth century, but an extended family. This would have included parents, children, relatives, and slaves, both male and female. The word household *says it better. The setting for Paul's letter to Titus is a household comprised of all kinds of people with all kinds of needs, and Titus is responsible for teaching them. He must adapt his instruction to their individual and particular needs.*

The instruction to be given is somewhat similar to the household codes of the day. Both Jews and Gentiles were familiar with these codes. The Stoics, the Jewish Essenes, and various Roman parties developed lists of do's and don'ts to guide their members. Some of these ethical instructions became subjects for the Greek theater, thus giving the people greater exposure to them. But there is an essential difference between the moral codes of ancient society and those of Christianity. The vice and virtue lists can only describe how people ought to live, whereas the Christian gospel of grace brings power to perform. When God commands, He gives the power to live out the command. The purpose of Christ's great redeeming sacrifice is to purify "a people who are his very own" (vs. 14). All the ancient virtue lists were powerless to impart the quality of life that Christ makes available to His followers.

It is behavior, conduct, and fine deeds that Paul stresses. The teaching must point toward the development of this distinctive lifestyle, and the striking contrast to the empty, futile lives of the masses will give the gospel a powerful impact. By their lifestyle, Christians adorn the doctrine of Christ, making it attractive and winsome.

∎ Getting Into the Word

Read Titus 2 several times. Then ask yourself the follow-ing questions. Keep your Timothy-Titus notebook close by for writing down your thoughts.

1. Reread the pastoral epistles, and find all of Paul's refer-ences to "sound doctrine" and similar terms. Examine the context of each one. What do you learn about the problems facing the second-generation Christian lead-ership? What does your study suggest about the role of Christian leadership? What does it imply about an ag-ing church? What does this suggest about the church today? What does it suggest about your denomination and your local congregation?

2. In verses 2 to 10 Paul addresses four groups of believ-ers. Outline the counsel for each group. What can we today learn from the counsel to each group?

3. Verses 11 to 14 provide a helpful yet concise statement on salvation. List the elements set forth in that passage. Then in a few sentences explain the meaning of each item in that list. In particular, it will be helpful to study the word *redeem* and *redeemed* in a concordance. Also study their meaning in Exodus and Leviticus. What can be determined about the meaning of *redeem*? Then go to the New Testament and read all the references to *redeem* and *redeemed*. In what ways does such a study enrich your understanding of Titus 2:14?

∎ Exploring the Word

Teaching Adapted to the Needs of the People

Paul told Titus that he must "teach [speak] what is in accord with sound doctrine" (vs. 1). The key word here is *laleō*, which means to talk, utter words, preach, say, speak, tell. Ministers of the gospel use the power of speech. The Anchor Bible makes an appropriate comment:

> How do these ministers fulfill their function? . . . Primarily by speaking. Their specific "ministry of the Word" is distinct from glorified verbosity, loquacity, gossiping. . . . "Apostles, prophets, teachers," etc., listen before they talk . . . learn and are sent before they teach . . . think before they pronounce, care for being understood rather than impose themselves upon people in need of edifying speech. . . . They are motivated by love of their neighbor rather than by the desire to show off a superior intelligence or status of their own. . . . They speak only when and because they have a most urgent message to convey. This message is called the "word of truth" or "the gospel" (Barth, 483).

The teaching must be in accord with sound doctrine (vs. 1). The word translated as "sound" suggests good health, to be well in body, to be incorrupt, wholesome. Doctrine, of course, is instruction, learning, information. There is a body of doctrine that is sound and true, which is recommended by the apostles and brought home to the heart by the Holy Spirit. These are the "trustworthy sayings" (1 Tim. 1:15; 3:1; 4:9; 2 Tim. 2:11; Titus 3:8). Preachers are not authorized to create their own message. The curriculum has already been decided by the Holy Spirit, the Supreme Teacher, who communicates this body of truth to the apostles.

"For what I received I passed on to you as of first importance" (1 Cor. 15:3), Paul said to the Corinthians. This is the "common faith" referred to in 1:4. The Old Testament instruction to keep the book of the law at hand is brought up to date (see Josh. 1:7-9). The Jerusalem Bible catches the meaning of the text well: "It is for you then to preach the behavior which goes with healthy doctrine" (vs. 1). Paul wants to see the Christians on the island of Crete develop a spiritually healthy lifestyle. Their doctrine is to shape and mold their character.

Now comes another of Paul's vice-and-virtue lists. In this case he addresses specific groups of people.

Older people. The older men are to be clear-headed and self-controlled. The word *nēphalios*, translated as "temperate," is

used only in the pastoral epistles (1 Tim. 3:2, 11; Titus. 2:2). Twice
it is used in advice to church elders and once to female associates
or deacons (1 Tim. 3:11). The warning is against the abuse of
wine. The list makes the point that every senior believer is to
possess the same qualifications for service as the church elder. This
is the lofty ideal. The older brothers in the church are to have the
same commitment to truth and the same firm grip on the message—"sound in faith"—as the elder. The King James Version
uses *patience*. *Hupomonē*, the Greek word translated in verse 1 as
"endurance," is one of the great New Testament words, used some
thirty-three times. It means cheerful endurance, constancy, patient continuance, waiting.

The old men must keep their faith high in spite of advancing
years and their long wait for the Lord's return. They are to model
the very best attributes of the Christian lifestyle.

Older women. "Likewise, teach the older women to be reverent
in the way they live" (vs. 3). Older women have a special ministry.
The idea of vocation or calling for women has good precedent.
The prophetess Anna (Luke 2:36-38) seems to be the ideal. The
senior women should strive to manifest the characteristics of one
who is assigned to ministry. They should also use speech properly
in carrying out their ministry. They are "not to be slanderers"
(literally, accusers, from *diabolos*—diabolic). Pastors should hold
this calling before older women and encourage them to meet the
requirements for carrying out this ministry.

Young women. As an integral part of the church's teaching ministry, older women are to "teach what is good" (vss. 3, 4). Their
specialty is "home and family." The young women are their "stu-
dents." They in turn are to fulfill the greatest task of all, the preparation of the next generation of witnesses for Christ. Young married women are managers of the home. Their special ministry
must be recognized. The outcome of this teaching is well-ordered
families that are a credit to the faith "so that no one will malign
the word of God" (vs. 5). The Christian home is indispensable to
the church's mission.

Young men. Titus is to be a model to younger men (vss. 6-8). He
is to be self-controlled, honest, serious, wholesome in his speech,
etc. His example is to be so positive and his life so clear that no

one can gainsay him. The critics are watching like vultures for any little bit of inconsistency or indiscretion so they will have something to pounce on viciously, to make public, and thus bring embarrassment on the church. The word picture is also that of a malicious prosecutor who gathers his evidence and brings it to court only to discover, to his chagrin, that his case is weak (vs. 8). It is thrown out of court. In its larger cosmic setting, this is what finally happens to the charges brought by the accuser of the brethren in the final judgment (Rev. 12:10).

Slaves. "Teach slaves," Paul said, "to be subject to their masters" (vs. 9). Again, this is to be understood in the context of the household. Paul is dealing with what *is*, not with what *ought to be*. The household codes are practical instructions for the time being. In this instance they are rules for survival. The point is that slaves are recognized members of the household. Nor is their household just in the home where they happen to serve; Christian slaves are members of "God's household, which is the church of the living God, the pillar and foundation of the truth" (1 Tim. 3:15). Believing slaves have a new status before God. They are responsible members of the body of Christ and are accountable for its welfare and mission.

It is also to be kept in mind that slaves were among the Palestinian refugees who made their way to Crete. Perhaps they had been free persons in Palestine, and even wealthy, but now their fortunes are completely reversed. Paul's fear is that these unfortunate people may be infected with the insurrectionist views of religious zealots. The zealots (I am using the term broadly, not in its technical sense) had brought pain and suffering on their homeland. They claimed great zeal for Israel's religion and God, but they were actually terrorists and assassins.

Paul has had his experience with them (Acts 20:3; 23:12-22). He sees that they are not super patriots but firebrands. The last thing he wants is to see the Cretan Christian community under suspicion of being Jewish insurrectionists. Therefore, slaves, though equal before God, must not act unwisely. They must not be carried away by secular "liberation" theologies.

The zealots sought out slaves and other unhappy people and used them to further their own evil plots. Not a few false prophets urged their followers to riot and perished with them.

If the slaves will follow the wise course that the apostle urges Titus to teach, they will make the doctrine of Christ attractive (vs. 10). The world will come to see that Christians are quality people, sober, sensible, reliable, and trustworthy. Paul's first concern is mission, proclamation, evangelism. Every member of God's household is responsible for mission. In fact, the church was organized for missionary purposes. Wherever the church is found, there is—or should be—found mission. "As the fire exists by burning," says Emil Brunner, "so the church exists by mission."

It is interesting to observe that slaves are the only group in the household that the apostle specifically mentions as making "the teachings about God our Savior attractive" (vs. 10).

One further observation needs to be made about Paul's use of household codes, not only in Titus but throughout his epistles. These codes are directed specifically to the group for whom they are intended. Each member of the household is to respond voluntarily and freely. The husband is not to force his wife to submit, nor is the master counseled to demand submission of the slave. The word *hupotassō*, translated as "submission," "obedience," or "subjection," appears first in Luke 2:51, where Jesus is spoken of as being obedient to His parents. As adult members of the community, each is to respond in the same manner and spirit in which the instruction is set forth. Submission is voluntary. The framework is love and mutual respect. The example is Jesus, whose submission was voluntary and in harmony with the will of God.

What Grace Teaches

"The grace of God that brings salvation has appeared to all men" (vs. 11). This salvation was made visible in a Person. It is not difficult to see that this is Paul's favorite theme. For him, grace is not an abstract theory. Grace is personified in the Saviour, the Lord Jesus Christ. "We have seen his glory, the glory of the one and only Son, who came from the Father, full of grace and truth. . . . Grace and truth came through Jesus Christ" (John 1:14, 17).

This grace "teaches us to say 'No' to ungodliness and worldly passions" (vs. 12). One ancient baptismal formula requires the candidate to say, "I renounce you, Satan, and all your service and all your works" (Quinn, 164). Each member of the household has been given the power of choice. Each one can say No! By the grace of God, all are to "live self-controlled, upright and godly lives in this present age" (vs. 12). Discipline—discipleship—is central to the post-baptismal life of the believer.

Grace is a one-word theology, "beyond all computation" (White, *Sons and Daughters of God*, 11). And as a truly great word symbol should, it points to supreme reality. Jesus is that reality. All that we can ever hope to know about God and truth, all that we need to know about God and reality, is already revealed in Jesus of Nazareth. Robert Oppenheimer used to say, "The best way to send a message is to wrap it up in a person." Jesus is God's last word, His ultimate communication.

While it is completely free, grace must not be cheapened. Deitrich Bonhoeffer, the theologian-martyr, coined the phrase "cheap grace." He called cheap grace "the deadly enemy of our church. We are fighting for costly grace" (see Kelly and Nelson, 324). Bonhoeffer used strong language, rebuking the church of his day for selling grace on the market

> like a cheapjack's wares. . . . In such a church the world finds a cheap covering for its sins; no contrition is required, still less any real desire to be delivered from sin. Cheap grace therefore amounts to a denial of the living Word of God, in fact a denial of the Incarnation of the Word of God. Cheap grace means the justification of sin without the justification of the sinner (see Kelly and Nelson, 324, 325).

The people of God in every age have been tempted to accept a cheapened form of grace through forgiveness without obedience, or, at the opposite extreme, a new version of salvation by works. But when the church has succumbed to either heresy, it has turned on us "like a boomerang" (see Kelly and Nelson, 327). What is being offered to us by a wise and loving God is the genuine article, the real thing, "the grace that brings salvation" (vs. 11). This is the way Christians are to live as they "wait for the blessed hope—the glorious appearing of our great God and Saviour, Jesus Christ" (vs. 13).

Seventh-day Adventists, along with fellow Christians, have struggled to maintain this biblical balance between law and grace. How does obedience figure into the salvation equation? Ellen White's comments on the above passage are to the point: "He [Paul] bids Titus instruct the church that while they should trust to the merits of Christ for salvation, divine grace, dwelling in their hearts, will lead to the faithful performance of all the duties of life" (*Sanctified Life*, 87). "The law, obeyed, leads men to deny 'ungodliness and worldly lusts,' and to 'live soberly, righteously, and godly in this present world' " (*The Acts of the Apostles*, 505).

The Blessed Hope

Christians live in anticipation. They have something to look forward to—"the glorious appearing [*epiphaneia*] of our great God and Savior, Jesus Christ" (vs. 13). This theme is repeated often in Paul's writings. The word *epiphaneia* usually refers to the advent of Christ, whether His first or His second coming, accompanied by brightness. It is used five times in the pastoral epistles (1 Tim. 6:14; 2 Tim. 1:10; 4:1, 8; Titus 2:13). In all but one instance (2 Tim. 1:10), the reference is to Christ's second coming. The one other use of *epiphaneia* in the New Testament is in connection with the "unmasking" of the "lawless one" (2 Thess. 2:8), the outlaw par excellence, and his destruction "by the splendor of his [Christ's] coming [*epiphaneia*]."

Paul appropriated *epiphaneia* and used it to describe the literal, visible, glorious manifestation of the Saviour. He was seen once in bodily form. He will be seen again in power and great glory at the end of the age. Paul names this event "the blessed hope." All Christians await this glorious appearance (vs. 13). It is the climax and culmination of the plan that was hidden in ages past and became a major theme of the apostles' preaching—and indeed of the church's proclamation throughout the centuries.

The appearing of the Saviour is the "blessed hope" of the faith community. The word for hope is *elpis*, which means to anticipate, usually with pleasure, expectation, and confidence. As the hymn says it, "How cheering is the Christian's hope, While toiling here below! It buoys us up while passing through this wilderness of woe." This has been true of Christians in every generation and will continue to be so until the second coming.

Redeeming Sacrifice—Redeemed People

The sacrifice of Jesus literally "redeem[s] us from all wickedness" (vs. 14). This includes a catalog of sins that make up the various vice lists, generally categorized as "ungodliness and worldly passions" (vs. 12). These words cover a great deal of territory. The point is, the one great sacrifice of Jesus addresses the sin problem on all fronts, the sin of the world and the sins of each individual in it.

This rescue is carried out so that God can make us "a people that are his very own" (vs. 14). The idea of the *laos* (people of God, or laity) is an apt word picture of the relationship that exists between the body of believers and their Supreme Commander, Jesus Christ. In the early days of the empire, there was a special bond between a general and his soldiers that gave the soldier in the field status. This is the relationship that should exist between God and His people.

God intends to have a visible people (*laos*) on earth who reflect His character and attributes. He wants to bless all nations through them. "Now," God said through Moses, "if you obey me fully and keep my covenant, then out of all nations you will be my treasured possession" (Exod. 19:5). Peter states it again, this time referring to the church: "You are a chosen people, a royal priesthood, a holy nation, a people belonging to God, that you may declare the praises of him who called you out of darkness into his wonderful light. Once you were not a people, but now you are the people of God; once you had not received mercy, but now you have received mercy" (1 Pet. 2:9, 10). The *laos*, God's redeemed people, are eager to do good works, and these good works are significant. They make the grace of God visible in a way that human beings can begin to understand it.

The New Testament church is God's covenant community, the

new Israel. They enjoy all the rights and privileges of the covenant. They are the apple of God's eye, His prized possession. They are a kingdom of priests whose function is to assist the one great High Priest as His representatives on earth.

Paul has now finished outlining what Titus is to teach. The message is trustworthy; its source is God. His commission is also from God. With this assurance, Titus is to "encourage and rebuke with all authority" (vs. 15). "No one is to question it" (vs. 15, Jerusalem Bible).

■ Applying the Word

1. Suppose you were asked to serve on a committee to evaluate your church—its spiritual formation, its various ministries, and its role and function. Where would you begin? What place should the pastoral epistles be given in the assignment? What underlying principles do you see in your study of Timothy and Titus that you have found helpful in understanding the work of the church? What ministry has God given you? How would you evaluate it in light of the instruction in Titus 2?

2. What can and should the church be doing to make the leadership selection process more inclusive, as Paul seems to be doing in Titus 2? Why do you think no specific instructions are given to young women in this chapter? What can we do to facilitate the homemaker role being understood as a ministry equal to any other?

3. What are we doing to make the doctrine of Christ more attractive to our neighbors and friends? How can we demonstrate that biblical teachings and correct doctrines do not make one harsh and unsympathetic? We have already mentioned the greatest argument in favor of Christianity. Do you remember what it is?

■ Researching the Word

1. Use a concordance to look up everything Paul says in his epistles about Christians who are slaves of earthly masters. Prepare a list of each point he makes, and put a

check mark by each item each time he repeats it. What does Paul emphasize the most? How can his advice be harmonized with the principle that God wants all people to be free? Would Paul have been an abolitionist in America during the early 1800s, before the slaves were set free? Explain your answer. What part of his advice is still relevant in a world in which slavery has largely been outlawed?

2. Look up all the occurrences of the word *grace* in the New Testament, or select certain books of the New Testament, and look up the word *grace* in them. What does *grace* mean? What does it accomplish? What advice do the New Testament writers give for making grace real in your life?

3. Prepare a Bible study on the second coming of Christ that emphasizes the meaning of Christ's coming for Christians. If you are not familiar with the major New Testament texts on this subject, you can find them in the *Seventh-day Adventist Bible Dictionary* under "Second Coming of Christ."

■ Further Study of the Word

1. For insight on salvation as experienced in justification and sanctification, see *Seventh-day Adventists Believe . . .* , 110-113; Siegfried H. Horn, et. al., *Seventh-day Adventist Bible Dictionary*, s.v. "justification" and "sanctification."

2. For a greater understanding of the second coming of Christ, see Ellen G. White, *The Great Controversy*, 299-304, 635-652; Francis D. Nichol, ed., *Seventh-day Adventist Bible Commentary* on Matthew 24, 25; 1 Corinthians 15:50-58; 1 Thessalonians 4:13-18; 2 Thessalonians 2:1-12; Revelation 6:12-17; 19:11-21.

CHAPTER TWELVE

Doing What Is Good

Titus 3

The apostle's vision in his letter to Titus is the formation of a powerful witnessing fellowship that "has it all together"—sound, wholesome doctrine incorporated into lifestyle; a community where the claims of law and grace are integrated and balanced; a vibrant company of the redeemed who live by grace and are distinguished by fine deeds, "eager to do what is good." It may come as a surprise to some that the foremost exponent of the grace of God is very much into good works. (The Anchor Bible uses the expression "fine deeds.") In the conclusion of his epistle to Titus, Paul zeroes in on the results, the outcome of grace, which is good works. This really should not surprise us, because close by the great declaration of salvation by grace in Ephesians 2:8, 9 comes the balancing phrase in verse 10: "For we are his workmanship, created in Christ Jesus to do good works, which God prepared in advance for us to do."

The apostle's wish is that the church will be a force to be reckoned with. He envisions a people through whom God's universal purposes will be accomplished. It is an exciting vision. No one could ever accuse Paul of not having a dream!

■ Getting Into the Word

Read Titus 3 several times. Then examine the following questions and suggestions.

1. Itemize each side of the great before-and-after contrast in verses 3 to 8. Compare these lists with Ephesians 2:1-10. What is the same? What is different? Why does

Paul use similar approaches in so many of his epistles?

2. What does Paul mean by "washing of rebirth and renewal by the Holy Spirit" in verse 5? In what ways do Ephesians 5:26 and John 3:1-8 help us understand that passage?

3. In verse 8 Paul once again speaks about being justified by grace. Review Romans 3, 4. How does being justified by grace relate to law? If salvation is all of grace apart from works, why does Paul place such strong emphasis on good works, especially in Titus? How many times is good works or doing good mentioned in Titus? How can the two emphases of grace and good works be harmonized?

4. List what can be learned from Paul's final remarks in Titus 3:12-15. What do such sections in each of his letters tell us about Paul?

■ Exploring the Word

Healthy Attitude

Many of the dispersed Jews were seething with discontent. Some of them probably had been members of revolutionary societies. Palestine, about the time of the writing of the pastoral epistles, was racked by violence. The groups that fomented these civil disturbances were loosely referred to as "zealots." Their zeal was worthy of a better cause. That is why Paul told Titus to "remind the people to be subject to rulers and authorities, to be obedient, to be ready to do whatever is good" (vs. 1).

It may be that the letter to Titus was written against a backdrop of house churches that were upset by "Christian" zealots disguising their revolutionary sentiments as zeal for the law. The people of God have a higher mission. They are not to slander anyone, even enemies. Unlike the firebrands of the day, they are to respect authorities (see also Rom. 13:1-6; 1 Tim. 2:1-4). They must be model citizens in the community. They should be ready to do any honorable work (vs. 1). Paul gave similar counsel to the Thessalonians (2 Thess. 3:10).

Though not reliable in every respect, Josephus and other historians of the time paint a rather credible picture of the spirit of these "mobsters." The Anchor Bible sketches a description based on Josephus's account and other sources. The so-called zealots are "angry enthusiasts and extremists, embodying a terrifying combination of cold-blooded politics and hotheaded piety, they chose their name shrewdly so that it justified in advance every act that they would perform" (Quinn, 174). They were contemptuous of all people, provoked fights, and were quarrelsome and vengeful.

Paul exhorts the members of the Christian household "to slander no one" (vs. 2). *Blasphēmeō* is the word translated "slander" by the NIV (KJV: "speak evil"). *Blasphēmeō* means to vilify, to speak impiously, to rail on, to revile, to defame. Christians are not to rail on neighbors or authorities. Their conversation is always to be well-ordered, "seasoned with salt" (Col. 4:6; see also James 3:5, 6, 8, 9; 1 Pet. 3:10; Jude 1:10).

Christian demeanor is "to be peaceable and considerate, and to show true humility to all men" (vs. 2). To show is to demonstrate, to make manifest. It takes deeds and actions to do this. The apostle keeps emphasizing this outward manifestation of what has happened on the inside. He comes down hard on what is seen in the life. Words and deeds are the test (see also Matt. 12:37; Eccl. 12:14; Rev. 20:13).

Zeal, zealousness, zealot—these are not bad words. Originally, the word *zealot* simply meant one who is zealous for God's law. Jesus had tremendous zeal for His Father's house (John 2:17). Every Jew was in a sense a zealot. The law was God's legacy to Israel. But, as has been observed, in verses 1, 2 the apostle is targeting the radical Zealot party and its sympathizers. He wants to disassociate the Christian community on Crete from these firebrands, to put as much distance between the zealots and the church as possible. The true zealot is distinguished by good deeds done for the benefit of all people (vs. 2). This is the attitude that should characterize every follower of Christ.

Misguided zealots and hotheads have caused the church untold trouble and pain throughout the centuries. Luther had his problems with them. The mass murder of the Huguenots of France was precipitated by a foolish handbill written in excessive language that attacked the predominant religious authority. One of these handbills was delivered to the king's palace. It was actually placed in his bedroom! The monarch, who had tried to be fair toward Protestants, was outraged and provoked to action. Individual Christians should be ready to make the supreme witness. That is the meaning of the word *martyr*. But individual Christians are never at liberty to place their own lives, the lives of others, the welfare of the community, or the cause of truth (above all) in jeopardy through precipitous actions.

Unfortunately, some Christians still believe that God wants them to attack those they disagree with. While it is true that we must wage vigorous warfare against the enemy, we are to do so with spiritual weapons (2 Cor. 10:3, 4). Some in our own day would bring on the time of trouble ahead of time by provoking the powers that be (secular or religious) or by provoking the community as a whole through injudicious methods of spreading the truth. Paul's counsel to Titus is timeless and timely—to "slander no one, to be peaceable and considerate, and to show true humility toward all men" (vs. 2).

Freedom From Past Slavery

Life without God is for Paul abject slavery. "At one time we too were . . . enslaved" (vs. 3), he says, and he includes his own pre-Damascus experience. He is talking about slavery to "all kinds of passions and pleasures" (vs. 3). This principle is clearly spelled out in Romans 6:16. In his early life, Paul, along with his fellow Israelites, tried in vain to obtain salvation by works, but instead of peace he found inner conflict and misery. Paul speaks of the inability of these works of the law to produce righteousness. It is a quicksand experience, and greater striving only makes the situation more hopeless. It is a life without love. "We lived in malice and envy, being hated and hating one another" (vs. 3). The recital is so gloomy and oppressive that the reader wants relief. The apostle makes us uncomfortable. Is there any way out?

This is another of Paul's teaching devices. We are drawn into the scene. His experience becomes everyone's biography. The picture is of a rebellious teenager refusing counsel or a strong-willed child who throws temper tantrums to get his way. Giving in to him only makes the next tantrum more violent. Furthermore, there is the unbridled lust and passion of addicts—the sex-crazed deviant, the alcoholic wallowing in the gutter, the drug addict lying in a flophouse. This is not a pretty picture. It is disgusting and repulsive, just as the apostle wants it to be. He is trying to awaken revulsion. Nothing in Paul's past life titillates or awakens in him a hankering for its consuming pleasures. It holds no charms for him. He wants the Cretan Christians to make a complete break with the past—no turning back. And he fears lest the description of his pre-baptismal life, if it is not stark enough, will awaken desire.

"But when the kindness and love of God our Savior appeared" (vs. 4). Kindness, love, and mercy, showed up in the person of Jesus Christ, who is God with us. This public, visible manifestation of Deity radically changes out past, present, and future. His appearing (the incarnation) is powerful and meaningful in the lives of individuals. God invests all heaven in the appearance of His Son, who invades history and changes the hopeless equation that had so negatively impacted the human situation. Before the "appearance" became a reality in their lives, all believers had a common history. They were, as the apostle puts it in Ephesians 2:12, "without hope and without God in the world." What made the difference? The appearance of the kindness and love of the Saviour (vs. 4). Here again is grace personified. Kindness and love describe all of God's gracious acts. Jesus is the epitome, the embodiment of a kind and gracious God.

Paul says of Jesus that "he saved us" (vs. 5), meaning, literally, that He delivered us and preserved us. The connotation is of a dramatic and decisive rescue, a miraculous intervention. The reclamation is so complete that the former life no longer has any power over the believer. He or she is no longer a prisoner, no longer a victim of the past. Moved by His great mercy, God initiates this saving, liberating action. But no righteous works of ours made Him kindly disposed to us. In fact, the opposite is the case. He was drawn to us because our situation was so hopeless! "He saw me plunged in deep distress, He flew to my relief," wrote Charles Wesley. Mercy suits our case better than any other divine attribute.

"There is no appreciating God's saving work," says Jerome

Quinn, "until men and women have demolished root and branch any presupposition about having earned this rescue because of the good things that human beings have first done for their God" (Quinn, 215, 216). Ellen White speaks clearly also: "Let no one take the limited, narrow position that any of the works of man can help in the least possible way to liquidate the debt of his transgression. This is a fatal deception" (Francis D. Nichol, ed., *SDA Bible Commentary*, 6:1071). It is all of grace.

Paul goes on to explain how Jesus saved us *"through the washing"* (vs. 5). This washing is baptism, and more. Baptism is a port of entry for the kingdom of God. It is the door into a brand new existence. It gives the believer a whole new world to explore, a new life to live, with new goals, new objectives, and a new agenda. There is rebirth, and there is constant renewal (vs. 5). Baptism is the initiating bath. The Spirit superintends the project, which begins in grace and concludes in glory. The washing or bath is intended to be a one-time event. After entry, however, there is continual renewal. The new life must be sustained.

The word translated "rebirth" (*paliggenesia*) is used in only one other place in Scripture—Matthew 19:28, where Jesus speaks of the kingdom restored (KJV: "the regeneration"). *Anakainōsis*, the word for renewal, indicates a renovation. It also appears only one other time, in Romans 12:2, where the apostle speaks about the renewing of the mind. This major cleansing and the subsequent post-baptismal renewal/renovation are described as justification and sanctification, although the scriptural description is not as precise as some would like to make it. It is sometimes difficult to tell where one ends and the other begins.

The Holy Spirit is the effective divine agent, as the phrase "by the Holy Spirit" suggests. He (the Spirit) was "poured out on us generously" (vs. 6). All the New Testament writers, especially Paul, delight in the superabundance of God. He provides "immeasurably more than all we ask or imagine" (Eph. 3:20). Jesus assures us, however, that all of this is within our reach. "How much more will your Father in heaven give the Holy Spirit to those who ask him" (Luke 11:13)! The work of the Spirit is immeasurably great. He brings all other blessings in His train.

The people Paul is addressing through Titus have already "been justified by his grace" (vs. 7). Justification is one of Paul's favorite themes. In this passage he is applying his theology. This is not textbook doctrine but the everyday kind of religion that touches us where we are. Paul is saying in effect, You have already been made right with God. The account is paid. This opens the way for you to be made heirs. Heirs have something to look forward to—their inheritance. For the Cretan believers, this is the prospect of eternal life.

This is the last of those "trustworthy sayings" (vs. 8) that Paul uses to tie off an argument or train of thought. These are the things Titus is to stress in his teaching and preaching. This is what constitutes the "deposit, the common faith." This message is to be preached in such a way as to encourage believers to "devote themselves to doing what is good" (vs. 8). Titus is to be intentional in this respect. He must teach with purpose, with the desired outcome in view.

The pastoral epistles insist that believers not only do good works but that they do them in a way that makes them attractive. Doing good works with grace! Good works then become allies with grace in producing the kind of character that will commend the doctrine of Christ to unbelievers. Good works have a missionary purpose. "In the same way, let your light shine before men, that they may see your good deeds and praise your Father in heaven" (Matt. 5:16). "Grace deeds" make the Christian life attractive.

People who follow Paul's inspired instruction will be vibrant, growing Christians, wholesome in their experience. This kind of community will make the church a body of light, "like stars in the universe" (Phil. 2:15). This brand of Christianity is not just busy work, works done for merit, for works that create tension cause strain and anxiety. *Fulfillment* is the word that comes nearer to saying it adequately. "These things are excellent and profitable for everyone" (vs. 8).

Duty to Warn the Divisive

Social scientists would tell us that in any sizable group there will be a few persons who are likely to exhibit certain kinds of disruptive behaviors. Ellen White observes, "Men and women who, with their different organizations, are brought together in church capacity have peculiarities and faults" (*Testimonies for the Church*, 3:359). The fanatic chooses one aspect of truth to the exclusion of others and insists that the entire fellowship follow suit. When that is not done, this person becomes irrational and belligerent. Paul's counsel is to warn such a person "once, and then warn him a second time," and then "have nothing to do with him" (vs. 10).

The health and prosperity of the church are at stake. The troublemaker must be rebuked and warned. Ellen White continues her observation, referring now to an actual case:

> As these [objectionable character traits] are developed, they will require reproof. If those who are placed in important positions never reproved, never rebuked, there would soon be a demoralized condition of things that would greatly dishonor God. . . . Principle should be brought to bear upon the one who needs reproof, but never should the wrongs of God's people be passed by indifferently (*Testimonies for the Church*, 3:359).

This is the toughest assignment a church leader can take on. In saying that the divisive member is to be warned once, and then a second time, and "after that have nothing to do with him" (vs. 10), Paul means that the church must take strong action, clear and positive. It *must* be done. "One, only one, such element, if countenanced in the church, will destroy its peace, its unity, and its prosperity" (White, *Manuscript Releases* 12:282). Pliant Aaronic types are not the ones to handle such a crisis, nor are the impulsive, sword-wielding Peter types any more suitable. "And who is equal to such a task?" (2 Cor. 2:16).

The divisive person comes under the judgment of God and the church by virtue of his refusal to accept counsel. He has turned his ear from hearing and has thus invoked judgment on himself. He has pronounced himself incorrigible. The great concern of church leaders and members must be to save the body from confusion. False sympathy with the divisive person is out of order because, as Paul says, "You may be sure that such a man is warped and sinful; he is self-condemned" (vs. 11).

A Personal Word and Farewell

Paul saves his personal concerns for the last. Yet even in this section of the letter, matters of practical godliness and gospel order control his pen. There is an administrative item: "As soon as I send Artemas and Tychicus to you, do your best to come to me at Nicopolis" (vs. 12). Some denominations have called this the "distribution of labor." Churches must be cared for according to their present needs. Assignments must be made. Details such as travel arrangements and hospitality have to be handled. "Do everything you can to help Zenas the lawyer and Apollos on their way and see that they have everything that they need" (vs. 13).

Paul's final remarks resemble the brusk, staccato instructions of an executive memo. Even in farewell he cannot keep from reinforcing his former comments on the necessity of good works. He is still anxious that the people work hard to "provide for daily necessities and not live unproductive lives" (vs. 14).

Paul is an example in team ministry, inclusive leadership. He uses the first person plural, but not in the editorial sense. The man who was "caught up to the third heaven" (2 Cor. 12:2-6) still identifies with little people. For all his royal experiences in Christ and his special appointment, he is never imperious. "Greet those who love us in the faith" (vs. 15). Everything is in the context of the fellowship, which must be strengthened and maintained. Feelings of family and belonging are important. The Pauline benediction falls softly, like gentle rain on the earth. The disciples who receive his words are encouraged and refreshed. "Grace be with you all" (vs. 15).

■ Applying the Word

1. Paul urges upon Christians what some would refer to as civic responsibility. What does this say to you about voting? What principles guide the Christian who chooses to exercise this privilege? Does this suggest that Christians should become involved in protest marches and rallies? Explain your answer.

2. Throughout the pastoral epistles, Paul expresses his fear

that the Word of God and the Christian community may be brought into disrepute by rash or foolish actions on the part of an individual church member or a group. When this happens today, what can the church do? What kind of PR program would you put in place to improve the church's image in the community?

3. What can we learn from Paul's counsel on handling a divisive person? What are the underlying principles? How does this apply to today's church? What steps would you take in moving toward resolution? In what ways does the biblical counsel relate to current "conflict resolution" strategies? How does Paul prepare us for the possibility of failure in these extremely difficult cases? How can we make discipline redemptive rather than punitive? What is the ultimate purpose of church discipline (see 2 Tim. 2:25, 26)?

4. What is the function of footwashing in the post-baptismal life? When is rebaptism in order? Using the "door" or "port of entry" as a valid working metaphor, what should be the criteria, the indication, that rebaptism is called for? How would you counsel a person who asked your advice regarding rebaptism? How can one determine whether a particular sin warrants rebaptism or whether the footwashing ordinance is sufficient? How does Peter's experience in John 13:4-10 and Jesus' response inform the discussion?

■ Researching the Word

1. Use a concordance to find as many New Testament references as possible to temptations involving the emotions and the passions of the body—adultery, fornication, envy, hatred, anger (see also malice and wrath), etc. Read several verses before and after each one to get the context. What practical suggestions do the Bible writers offer for overcoming these temptations of "the flesh"?

2. Look up the last few verses of each of Paul's letters to churches and individuals (including the entire sixteenth

chapter of Romans). What do these passages suggest about Paul's relationships with people and churches? What is his attitude toward them? What does he expect of them? What practical application do you see in these passages for today's pastors in their relationship with churches? What practical application is there for members in dealing with pastors?

■ Further Study of the Word

1. For more on baptism, see Siegfried H. Horn, et. al., *Seventh-day Adventist Bible Dictionary*, 118, s.v. "baptism."
2. For a better understanding of the relationship between faith and works, see Ellen G. White, *Faith and Works*, 47-50.
3. For information on the unwise actions of certain Protestants in France that precipitated a crisis for all Protestant Christians, see Ellen G. White, *The Great Controversy*, 224, 225.